THE END OF BANKING

THE END OF BANKING

MONEY, CREDIT, AND THE DIGITAL REVOLUTION

JONATHAN MCMILLAN

Published by
Zero/One Economics GmbH
Zurich, Switzerland

Cover, book design, and illustrations by Marcel Bamert
Index by Sylvia Coates

The use of general descriptive names, registered names, trademarks, etc. in this book does not imply, even in the absence of specific statement, that such names are exempt from the relevant protective laws and regulations and therefore free for general use. All quotations in this book are used for illustrative or critical purposes only, and the words quoted remain the copyright of the respective copyright holders.

Although the author and publisher have made every effort to ensure that the information in this book was correct at press time, the author and publisher do not assume and hereby disclaim any liability to any party for any loss, damage, or disruption caused by errors or omissions, whether such errors or omissions result from negligence, accident, or any other cause. The author and publisher have no responsibility for the persistence or accuracy of URLs for any websites referred to in this book and do not guarantee that any content on such websites is, or will remain, accurate or appropriate.

For more information about this book, visit:
www.endofbanking.org

ISBN-13   978-3-9524385-1-0 (Paperback)

First Edition, 2014

10 9 8 7 6 5 4 3 2 1

Contents

─────────────── PART ONE ───────────────
Banking in the Industrial Age

─────────────── PART TWO ───────────────
Banking in the Digital Age

─────────────── PART THREE ───────────────
A Financial System for the Digital Age

List of Illustrations

List of Acronyms

ABCP	asset-backed commercial paper
ABS	asset-backed security
AIG	American Insurance Group
CDO	collateralized debt obligation
CDS	credit default swap
ETF	exchange-traded fund
FDIC	Federal Deposit Insurance Corporation
FFA	Federal Financial Authority
GDP	gross domestic product
LIBOR	London Interbank Offered Rate
MBS	mortgage-backed security
MMMF	money market mutual fund
OTC	over-the-counter
QIS	quantitative impact study
SEC	U.S. Securities and Exchange Commission
SPV	special purpose vehicle
TARP	Troubled Asset Relief Program

Preface

A lot of books claim to explain the problems with banking, but most of them fail to reach the essence of the matter. Some authors interpret the financial crisis of 2007–08 as a story of greedy bankers scamming innocent widows and orphans. Scandalous stories can be entertaining to read, but identifying unchangeable aspects of human nature as the root of all evil falls short. It will not prevent the next financial crisis. Neither will minor regulatory patches, which have been the standard answer to banking crises by many economists and politicians. The current problems with banking are deeply entrenched within the financial system. Fundamental change is needed, and some economists have indeed reverted to radical reform proposals that were originally developed decades ago. However, while old theories have valuable lessons to teach, we found that old solutions fail to solve today's problems with banking.

Disappointed by the existing approaches toward banking and its problems, we decided to write this book. It proved to be a formidable challenge. The difficulty lies in the elusiveness of banking. Banking can appear in various forms. By generalizing our understanding of it, we have been able to identify the basic financial techniques that are common to all forms of banking—whether it is performed by medieval goldsmiths or by today's managers at investment banks. We found that banking was a sensible way to organize the financial system in the industrial age, but it got out of control with the rise of information technologies. The financial crisis of 2007–08 was an inevitable consequence of banking in the digital age.

Revealing the deficiencies of today's banking system is only a first step. The main purpose of this book is to show how to restore a functioning financial system. How the financial system is organized is of an importance that cannot be exaggerated. The organization of the financial system affects the stability, the productivity, and the distributive justice of the economy. This is why the largest part of this book is concerned with outlining a financial system for the digital age.

Although *The End of Banking* is primarily addressed to our colleagues in economics and finance, any interested reader can follow the arguments. We have avoided jargon as much as possible and have explained banking and its problems in a nontechnical way. Nevertheless, reading this book remains an intellectual journey, and we advise you to read it from start to finish if you have no background in economics or finance. For readers familiar with the matter, the first part is more of a refresher that might be skipped.

This book is the result of careful deliberation, and we have chosen its title for a good reason. Once the transformative potential of the digital revolution is understood, traditional ways to organize the financial system no longer appear sustainable. Calling for the end of banking might be considered presumptuous. We hope to convince you on the following pages that it is nothing but necessary.

Jonathan McMillan
August, 2014

THE END OF BANKING

Introduction

A financial system without banking is both desirable and possible. While banking once was a useful activity that provided essential economic functions, the digital revolution turned the tables. Banking slipped out of control because information technology rendered banking regulation ineffective. The financial crisis of 2007–08 heralded a new age of unconstrained banking. But the effects of the digital revolution on the financial system are twofold. We not only lost control over banking in the digital age, we also no longer need it. Information technology offers new possibilities that make banking redundant. Ending banking will mark the beginning of a modern financial system.

Calling for the end of banking might sound too simplistic to solve today's problems in the financial system. Such a notion likely stems from a vague definition of banking. Some label all activities undertaken by banks as banking. Others think of banking as a bundle of financial services such as asset management or securities underwriting. We adopt a macroeconomic perspective and define *banking* as the creation of money out of credit. This might sound odd to people unfamiliar with this field. Rest assured that we will explain banking in great detail. For the moment, it is important to note that banking is not confined to the institution that we call the bank, and not all the activities banks are engaged in are banking. Banking is not a business model, but a way to organize the financial system.

Money, Credit, and Prices

Every modern economy features two interdependent systems: the real economy and the financial system. The *real economy* consists of all activities and resources used for the actual production and distribution of goods and services. The *financial system* is a virtual system whose purpose becomes clear once we have discussed its two elements: money and credit.

Money is used for current payment. It is a medium for exchanging goods and services immediately. Trading with money is superior to primitive barter, as it does not require a double coincidence of wants: You do not need to find the one person who offers exactly what you need and needs exactly what you offer. Money frees people from basic subsistence production and allows them to specialize in producing more complex goods and services. As a medium of exchange, money allows a *decentralized economy*—that is, a decentralized coordination of activities in the real economy.[1]

Credit is used for deferred payment. With credit, the payment of money and the transfer of goods and services take place at different points in time. Credit enables an efficient allocation over time and is critical to bridge the time required for setting up capital-intensive production. A first-time farmer, for instance, can increase productivity with a tractor. With credit, the farmer can acquire a tractor even without having any wealth and before gathering in the first harvest. Once the first harvest is sold, the credit obligation can be settled. Credit facilitates capital accumulation and is essential for industrial production. It lays the foundation for a *capital-intensive economy*.

The purpose of the financial system is to support a decentralized and capital-intensive economy. Without money and credit—that is, without media for current and deferred payment—people would be constrained to subsistence production and barter. Moreover, the use of money and credit allows prices to form.[2]

Prices are the hinge between the financial system and the real economy. When people use money and credit for their economic activities, prices form. At the same time, the economic activities of people in the real economy are guided by prices. Without prices, coordination within a decentralized and capital-intensive economy is challenging, if not impossible. While credit and money can be interpreted as a mirror, prices are the reflection of the real economy in the mirror. Just as you cannot judge your appearance properly without a mirror, a decentralized and capital-intensive economy can only be grasped by looking at prices.[3]

The Organization of the Financial System

How well the financial system fulfills its purpose of supporting a decentralized and capital-intensive economy depends on the organization of its two elements. If money and credit are ill-designed, prices will be a bad guideline for economic activity—likewise, the reflection in a distorting mirror is a bad reference for reality. The coordination of decentralized activities becomes impaired, capital is wasted, and some people might receive unwarranted gains at the expense of others. It is hard to overstate the importance of getting the organization of the financial system right. How we organize money and credit has a major impact on the stability, productivity, and fairness of an economy.

As a virtual system, the financial system only exists in human imagination. What is acceptable as money, for instance, is either ruled by common practice or by law. The organization of the financial system is the result of human deliberation. It has always and everywhere been a matter of politics.

Money is easier to organize than credit. People only need to agree on something that takes over the function of money. The time dimension is less prominent than with credit. From an individual's point of view, a monetary transaction involves a short time period. Counterparties do not necessarily need to trust each other when using money in a transaction. Once society has reached agreement about what to use as money, sellers of goods can be rather confident that they are able to use the money in another transaction. Even basic societies can succeed in establishing a financial system with money.[4]

In contrast, the organization of credit is much more difficult. Lenders have to trust borrowers over years or even decades. The difficulties—but also the benefits—of credit increase with the amount of time it bridges. While a car mechanic can repay credit taken for a few tools within a couple of months, it takes years for a car manufacturer to repay credit taken for a modern factory. A modern factory is much more productive—it can produce several more cars per worker compared to the car mechanic. But who would be so trusting or have enough patience to hand over their savings for a repayment promise 10 years down the road?

Part One: Banking in the Industrial Age

The needs of people who could use credit and those who could offer credit differ. This mismatch between borrowers and lenders puts credit on the fringes. The introduction of modern accounting technology—that is, double-entry bookkeeping—and the rise of the constitutional state establishing a rule of law have provided the foundations for banking and marked the ascent of credit. Banking helped match the needs of borrowers and lenders. It was a major innovation in the organization of the financial system that allowed credit to thrive. Part One of this book explains the need for banking in the industrial age.

We defined banking as the creation of money out of credit. How banking creates money out of credit will become clear when we explain the mechanics of traditional banking. Traditional banking is the simplest form of banking and combines lending and safekeeping. On the one hand, banks extend credit to borrowers. On the other hand, banks enable lenders to make deposits that feel "as good as money."

The characteristics of bank deposits made it attractive for lenders to participate in credit. In turn, credit supply increased what fostered capital accumulation. Banking facilitated the realization of capital-intensive industrial projects that took decades to cover their initial investment.

The industrialization, characterized by increasing capital intensity, was enabled by a modern financial system. While the transition

period—the Industrial Revolution—was accompanied with personal hardship, the increased productivity of a capital-intensive economy alleviated poverty on an unprecedented scale in the history of
humankind.

Recall that the economy consists of two interrelated systems:
the real economy and the financial system. The industrialization in
the real economy was visible to everyone, as factories with smok-
ing chimneys were popping up all over. Due to this visibility of
capital investments, some have called the new economic regime
capitalism. The term *capitalism* refers to the real economy. The real
economy could, however, only become capital-intensive and develop at such a fast pace as a result of improvements of the financial system.[5]

Notwithstanding its contributions to a capital-intensive economy, banking comes with serious flaws. From time to time, banking breaks down. These events are called bank runs, and they have
plagued banking ever since it began. Bank runs repeatedly escalated
into full-blown banking panics that shook the financial system to its
very foundations. Banking panics impair the ability of the financial
system to coordinate economic activities. They massively distort
prices and lead to deep recessions in the real economy.[6]

Two particularly severe panics, in 1907 and 1929, prompted the
U.S. government to tackle the problems with banking by establishing a tight regulatory framework: Government guarantees prevented bank runs, and banking regulations such as capital requirements
restricted banks from abusing the government guarantees. The regulatory framework proved successful in the industrial age. Society
could enjoy the benefits of banking, and the regulatory framework
kept its problems in check.

Part Two: Banking in the Digital Age

Part Two of this book is about how banking got out of control in the
digital age. In the 1970s, information technology entered the stage
and marked the beginning of the digital revolution. While credit
had to be recorded on paper in the industrial age, financial insti-

tutions could now record credit electronically. With the advent of computers and electronic communication networks, credit became detached from banks' balance sheets. This had far-reaching consequences for the effectiveness of banking regulation.

New forms of banking emerged, and banks organized their activities such that regulation did not apply. Institutions such as money market mutual funds (MMMFs) started to perform banking over a complex network of balance sheets and outside the regulators' spotlight. Banking that is not or only lightly regulated is often called *shadow banking*. Within a few decades, shadow banking became more important than traditional banking.

The rise of shadow banking highlights that banking is not limited to banks. Although a legal definition of a bank can be straightforward, it is considerably harder to legally define banking. The boundary problem of financial regulation describes this legal elusiveness of banking. Eventually, the failure of regulators to get a grip on the boundary problem resulted in another banking panic: the financial crisis of 2007–08.

The crisis was far reaching and called for decisive action. Only government bailouts of unprecedented scale prevented a complete meltdown of the financial system. The course of action taken, however, came at great cost.

Since the financial crisis of 2007–08, too-big-to-fail institutions enjoy an implicit government guarantee of all their liabilities. At the same time, regulators are unable to effectively regulate them. In a world with fast-paced financial innovation, financial institutions can move banking anywhere where banking regulation does not apply. The boundary problem of financial regulation has become insurmountable with information technology. Regulators are set for a race they are bound to lose.

In the digital age, banking has got out of control. Government guarantees have become all-encompassing, but banking regulation is no longer effective. The banking system turned into a dysfunctional public–private project. Banking institutions make tremendous profits by taking excessive risks in good times, while the government absorbs the losses in bad times.

Part Three: A Financial System for the Digital Age

The rise of information technology undermined the regulatory approach with which society got banking under control in the industrial age. While technological progress is known for shaking up established institutions, it usually opens up new possibilities as well. This process is known as *creative destruction*.[7] Information technology not only destroyed the functionality of the banking system, it also enabled a new organization of money and credit. In Part Three of this book, we turn to the creative effects of information technology.

New technologies such as peer-to-peer lending, virtual marketplaces, and digital currencies have emerged. They have opened up new possibilities to satisfy the demand of households for liquid and safe lending opportunities, while still providing borrowers with long-term financing for risky projects. By analyzing the new possibilities in their entirety, it becomes evident that banking is no longer needed. Information technology enables the financial system to support a decentralized and capital-intensive economy without resorting to banking. Doing without banking does not compromise the convenience for households and nonfinancial companies to manage their financial affairs. In the digital age, banking has not only gotten out of control, it has also lost its reason for existence.

Even though banking is no longer needed, it will continue to dominate our financial system. The new possibilities to manage money and credit cannot prevail as long as unconstrained banking is possible. Banking with full government guarantees but without effective regulation remains too profitable from an individual perspective, despite the tremendous costs it imposes on society. This is why we have to end banking.

We are not the first to call for an end of banking. In the industrial age, economists proposed narrow banking, and recently, another proposal called limited purpose banking has been suggested. While both proposals aim to end banking as we do, they fail to account for the elusiveness of banking in the digital age. The boundary problem of financial regulation calls for a holistic approach: We have to address banking at the fundamental level of accounting. For this, we propose a systemic solvency rule that effectively and efficiently prevents banking. Our proposal nests both narrow banking and limited purpose banking without falling prey to the boundary problem.

Ending banking requires redefining the role of the public sector in the organization of money and credit. On the one hand, the public sector no longer has to uphold banking guarantees. We can abandon the stifling regulatory framework imposed because of these guarantees and instead rely on competitive forces to organize credit. On the other hand, monetary policy needs to be reconsidered, as today's central banking builds on banking. We discuss two new monetary policy tools that are particularly suited to support a functioning price system: the liquidity fee and the unconditional income.

Taking a look at the big picture at the end of Part Three, we realize how the functions of money and credit—providing a medium for current and deferred payment—are closely intertwined in a banking system. Furthermore, we see that the public and the private spheres are not separated either. The mingling of both functions and responsibilities distorts prices, resulting in misallocations in the real economy.

Ending banking will reestablish an operative financial system. In a financial system without banking, the functions of money and credit are separated and assigned to the public and the private spheres, respectively. This way, the financial system can provide for a functioning price system and support a decentralized and capital-intensive economy. The stability, productivity, and fairness of our economy will no longer be compromised by an outdated organization of the financial system.

The Scope of This Book

Before we continue, two remarks regarding the scope of this book are in order. First, *The End of Banking* refers to the economic history, the institutional details, and the economic data of the United States. We chose the United States for our exposition because it has been the dominant economy from the 20th century onward. The insights we derive, however, apply to all modern economies that rely on banking.

Second, we do not cover the transition from a banking system to a financial system without banking. We also refrain from discussing international issues and spillover effects that always arise when discussing reform proposals. Before thinking about how to implement a better financial system, we first have to define where to go. This is the objective of this book: To show that a financial system without banking is both desirable and possible.

------------------------------ NOTES ------------------------------

1. Despite the importance of money, economists rarely model the functions of money as a medium of exchange. Standard general-equilibrium models are basically barter economies. Some models featuring money explicitly, to name a few, are provided by Starr and Ostroy (1974), Kiyotaki and Wright (1989), Banerjee and Maskin (1996), and Lagos and Wright (2005).

2. The price system is usually considered to be a function of money only. In contrast, we consider the price system as a function of the financial system. It is the result of the use of both money and credit. Consequently, interest rates are subsumed under our notion of prices. Both money (as a medium of current exchange) and credit (as a medium of deferred exchange) contribute to the formation of prices in the economy. Thinking about the price system as a pure monetary phenomenon has led to distorted methods to measure prices, as they neglect the time dimension of prices (see Alchian and Klein 1973; Goodhart 2001).

3. Since prices are formed on markets, decentralized economies are sometimes called market economies. In what follows, we always use the term *decentralized economy*. Observe that centrally planned economies do not fully rely on a price system to allocate resources. Many economists have elaborated on potential issues arising with such a setup; see, for example, Mises (1920), Lange (1936), and Hayek (1945).

4. Menger (1892) was among the first to argue that money comes into existence without political coordination. For a theoretical model that analyzes how money can arise endogenously, see Kiyotaki and Wright (1989) and Banerjee and Maskin (1996). Note that we do not claim that a simple organization of money results in a good financial system, that is, one that supports a functioning price system.

5. Many economists attribute to banking and financial markets an important role in fostering capital accumulation and economic growth. Schumpeter (1926) and Gerschenkron (1962) were early advocates of the hypothesis that capital accumulation

is closely related to financial market development. King and Levine (1993) and Levine and Zervos (1998) found empirical evidence that supports a positive impact of financial development in general on economic growth. In another article, Levine (1997) remarked on the liquidity transformation of a modern financial system that "because the industrial revolution required large commitments of capital for long periods, the industrialization may not have occurred without [it]" (p. 692).

6. The distortive effects of banking on the price system are particularly important for economists of the Austrian School. Block and Garschina (1996), for instance, argue that banking creates distortions without contributing to the accumulation of productive capital.

7. *Creative destruction* is a term that goes back to Schumpeter (1950), who describes it as something that "revolutionizes the economic structure from within, incessantly destroying the old one, incessantly creating a new one" (p. 83).

PART ONE

Banking in the Industrial Age

1 The Need for Banking

In the industrial age, banking was a good way to organize the fundamental elements of the financial system: money and credit. In particular, banking was indispensable for credit to thrive. The term *credit* refers to the trust required between two parties to trade over time. One party is receiving goods, services, or money today by promising to provide the other party with goods, services, or money in the future. As such, credit is deferred payment.[1]

There are different forms of credit. The most common one is the *loan*. We define a loan as the temporary transfer of money. The person who receives money first and pays back later is called *borrower*. The person who gives money first and gets it back later is called *lender*. The price that the borrower pays the lender for receiving money first is the *interest*. In the case of a loan, the *interest rate* is measured as a percentage of the *notional amount*, which is the amount of money initially exchanged.[2] The borrower pays back the notional amount until *maturity*, the agreed-on end date of the loan. The total time between handing over the notional amount and the maturity date is called the *term to maturity*.

Addressing Information Asymmetries

People lend money because they hope to receive the full notional amount and some interest back at a future date. They hope to be better off in the future after granting a loan instead of keeping the money in their pockets. Borrowers think quite similarly. They think they are better off by having money today, even though they have to pay it back with interest tomorrow.

If we abstract from the time dimension, a loan would just be a mutual exchange of money. The time dimension is the defining characteristic of credit. Talking about credit involves time and uncertainty. This brings up a whole collection of problems.

Imagine that you would like to grant a loan. First, you have to find someone who is trustworthy and able to pay back the full notional amount with interest. Usually, you do not know much about the borrower's character and ability. Economists call this problem *hidden knowledge*. Furthermore, you can never be sure whether potential borrowers will use the money in a way that they will be able to pay you back later. This problem is called *hidden action*. At the maturity date, a further problem might arise. The world could have changed unfavorably over the course of the loan, and the borrower might not be able to keep up with payments. But the borrower might also pretend to be unable to pay just to keep the money. If you think this is the case, you would be well advised to investigate the borrower's financial situation. Such an investigation is likely to be costly, which is why economists talk about *costly state verification* in this context.

All of these problems ultimately arise because of information asymmetries. Put simply, *information asymmetries* mean that the borrower knows more than the lender. For everybody who has ever lent money, this concept is quite intuitive. Information asymmetries are at the bottom of all problems with credit. They allow, for instance, moral hazard. *Moral hazard* arises if someone can enjoy the benefits arising from a certain course of action while passing on some or all negative consequences to others. In the case of credit, borrowers can lie in order to obtain loans that benefit them but that they will not be able to repay. The negative consequences of not repaying the loan are borne by the lender.[3]

Information asymmetries nurture *credit risk*, which is the risk of loss for a lender if a borrower does not—or not fully—repay the loan. If you do not want to lose too much money, you somehow have to deal with credit risk when lending. The activities that mitigate credit risk are often summarized under the term *monitoring*.[4]

How can lenders monitor borrowers? First, lenders thoroughly assess the trustworthiness of potential borrowers. Lenders gather credit-relevant information about borrowers to assess the credit risk involved in lending money. Based on the expected credit risk, lenders grant a loan with suitable terms, or they refuse to lend money altogether. Second, lenders maintain a close relationship to borrowers over the lifetime of loans. They verify that borrowers stick to the rules of the loan contract — the *covenants*.

In addition, a lender often asks a borrower to put up an asset to secure the loan. The asset is then called *collateral,* and the loan is a collateralized loan. Collateral can come in a variety of forms. A mortgage, for instance, is a collateralized loan where real estate serves as collateral. By collateralizing loans, credit risk is lowered significantly. If the borrower does not live up to contractual promises, the lender can claim and sell the collateral to make up for the losses.

As we can see, successful lending always requires effort to build trust. Lenders are well advised to actively manage their relationship with borrowers; to use a Russian proverb: trust, but verify. Monitoring borrowers can successfully address problems arising from information asymmetries.

While banks monitor their borrowers, this activity is not the defining one for a bank. Many other financial institutions are also engaged in monitoring activities, for example, rating agencies or venture capital funds. Banks are unique in a different respect: They bridge the mismatching needs between lenders and borrowers.

Matching the Needs of Borrowers and Lenders

Monitoring provides the foundation for credit. However, monitoring alone is not sufficient. For credit to thrive, the differing needs of lenders and borrowers need to be matched.

Let us clarify this with an example. Imagine that Sarah wants to start her own coffee-roasting business. This business requires her to buy expensive equipment such as a coffee roaster. The savings of one single person are usually not enough to finance a coffee roaster. In addition, the investment only pays off after a long time. Sarah will have to sell her freshly roasted coffee for quite some time until she will have earned enough to redeem her initial investments.

This example illustrates two needs of typical borrowers. First, they require large loans—that is, loans with a large notional amount—because tools and machinery are expensive. Second, they prefer long maturities, as they need time to earn enough money to pay back the loan.

The needs of borrowers do not coincide with those of lenders. Typical lenders—such as households—tend to have only small amounts of money at their disposal to lend. Furthermore, lenders are typically risk-averse and reluctant to expose themselves to significant credit risk. To spread their risk, they wish to lend only a fraction of their available savings to a single borrower. In addition, lenders prefer to have quick access to their savings as their lives are inherently uncertain. A lender could lose her job, or be offered a great job in another city. In both cases, the lender needs immediate access to her money lent such that she can pay for expenses arising from these unexpected events.

In summary, borrowers usually prefer loans with a large notional amount and long maturity to undertake risky investments. Lenders prefer loans with a small notional amount and short maturity so that they will be exposed to as little risk as possible. Matching the differing needs of lenders and borrowers is the essence of banking. Before we explain the mechanics of banking in the next chapter, let us discuss the third function of banking.

Facilitating Transactions with Payment Services

Given the important role of banks in addressing information asymmetries and matching the needs of borrowers and lenders, you might think that banking originated from some early lenders. Notwithstanding this intuition, banking actually originated from payment service providers. The predecessors of banks were custodians who stored the gold and coins of their clients and offered payment services for them.[5]

Custodians can facilitate the payments of their customers, which makes the customers' lives much more convenient. A simple example clarifies this. Assume that Sittah, the merchant, buys a caravel from Nathan, the owner of a shipyard. Both own some gold coins, with which they entrusted a custodian named Bonafides for safekeeping. In this situation, Sittah and Nathan can advise Bonafides to move gold coins from Sittah's custody account to the one of Nathan. Only two changes in booking entries in Bonafides's accounting books are needed. First, Sittah's account is debited with the amount of gold needed to buy the caravel. Second, Nathan's account is credited with the same amount. This greatly facilitates the transaction. Otherwise, Sittah would have to get her gold coins out of Bonafides's vault and hand them over to Nathan, who would then hand them back over to Bonafides.

Such payment services are very useful and are offered today by banks. They operate an *accounting system of exchange*.[6] Your employer transfers your salary via check or bank transfer. If no such payment services existed, every transaction would need to be settled in cash. You can imagine how tedious this would be, in particular, if you bought something from someone living far away.

While the above example illustrates that a custodian can offer payment services, it is not self-evident why banks can. The safekeeping contract of custodians is fundamentally different from the deposit contract of banks. A bank is no custodian. In fact, banks intend to lend out the money entrusted with them. As a depositor, you *lend* money to your bank: You are a lender and the bank is a borrower. The bank can use the money that you deposited for any purpose it deems appropriate, for instance, to grant loans to businesses.

Of course, for you as a depositor, this deal seems to be less safe than the situation in which your banker just keeps your gold coins in the vault. Why should you prefer a deposit contract to a safekeeping contract? Deposits have one big advantage: Instead of having to pay for the safekeeping services, you usually earn interest on your deposit. This explains why deposit contracts are so attractive and why custodians eventually evolved into banks.

Although banks do not safe-keep depositors' money but lend it out, they offer payment services as if they were pure safekeepers. Depositors seem to have their cake and eat it, too. On the one hand, depositors lend money and earn interest on it. On the other hand, they still have ready access to it. Why does the loan to the bank (i.e., the deposit) feel "as good as money"? This is the miracle of banking.

NOTES

1. The term *credit* originates from the Latin verb *credere*, which means "to trust." This elegantly describes the essence of credit.

2. Some also use the term *principal* or *face value*.

3. Moral hazard plays a pivotal role in banking, as we discuss later. For a discussion of the different problems in the realm of credit that arise due to information asymmetries, see Freixas and Rochet (2008). Information asymmetries can also imply *adverse selection* problems. For a seminal article on adverse selection on credit markets, see Stiglitz and Weiss (1981).

4. See, for example, Hellwig (1991). Ex ante monitoring, that is, monitoring before actually granting a loan to prevent adverse selection of borrowers, is often called *screening*. We use the term *monitoring* comprehensively for all activities that mitigate problems arising with information asymmetries.

5. The word *bank* originates from the old Italian word *banca*, which refers to a table. In the early days of banking, money exchange was taking place on a table on which the different coins were put. Over time, the money changers also became custodians and offered safekeeping and payment services on coins (Rajan 1998). In early England, goldsmiths took over this function of safekeeping (Richards 1929).

6. See Fama (1980).

2 The Mechanics of Traditional Banking

We defined banking as the creation of money out of credit. Under *traditional banking* we understand the creation of money out of credit by depository institutions, which are often just called banks. Hence, our definition of banking cuts across many common definitions. Often, people use the term *banking* for all sorts of activities undertaken by banks. In our context, however, only activities that are related to the creation of money out of credit fall under the term *banking*. Neither does every activity undertaken by banks constitute banking, nor is banking an activity that is only undertaken by banks.

It follows from our definition that neither lending nor pure safekeeping constitutes banking. Banking is more sophisticated. It brings together both activities in a unique way. Doing so requires a balance sheet. The two-sided banking business requires double-entry bookkeeping. In contrast, lending and safekeeping in isolation could be done with single-entry bookkeeping.

Double-Entry Bookkeeping Is a Prerequisite for Banking

Double-entry bookkeeping emerged in Italy around the turn of the 14th century.[1] It differs from single-entry bookkeeping in that each and every transaction is recorded twice.[2] Double-entry bookkeeping has several advantages. One is that recording transactions twice increases the accuracy of accounting, because the bookkeeper always double-checks every transaction.

Moreover, double-entry bookkeeping makes it easier to track individual investments in a company and measure economic success. It allows for abstract thinking about the business processes and economic efficiency.[3] With double-entry bookkeeping, companies not only record their assets in stock, but also chart how these assets are financed. Companies using double-entry bookkeeping account for what they own and owe on a record called a balance sheet.[4]

A *balance sheet* reports the financial situation of a company at a given point in time, divided into two sides: the *asset side* and the *liability side*. Regarding the items listed on a balance sheet, we can broadly distinguish among assets, liabilities, and equity. Figure 2.1 illustrates a stylized balance sheet.

Asset Side		Liability Side	
100	Assets (e.g., cash holdings, real estate, loans granted)	Liabilities (e.g., loans taken out)	60
		Equity	40
100	Total	Total	100

Figure 2.1 Stylized balance sheet

Assets are all the physical, immaterial, and financial resources that a company has under its control, that is, everything the company owns. *Liabilities* are all obligations that a company has entered in the past, that is, everything the company owes. Liabilities are always some form of credit—for instance, a loan obtained in the past. *Equity* is an ownership claim and not a form of credit: It features no maturity, no fixed notional amount, and no predetermined interest payments. Nevertheless, equity is recorded on the liability side of the balance sheet. Why this is so becomes clear once we look at how the value of equity is calculated.

The *book value* of equity is given by the net value of the company. It is calculated by subtracting the total asset value from the total liability value.[5] If the value of equity is positive, the company is *technically solvent* (Figure 2.1 depicts the balance sheet of a technically solvent company). If the value of equity is negative, the company is *technically insolvent* (see Figure 2.2).[6]

Asset Side		Liability Side	
100	Assets	Liabilities	130
	(e.g., cash holdings,	(e.g., loans taken out)	
	real estate,		
	loans granted)		
		Equity	-30
100	Total	Total	100

Figure 2.2 *Stylized balance sheet of a technically insolvent company*

Asset Transformation Matches Lenders and Borrowers

The characteristics of assets and liabilities on balance sheets differ in three important dimensions. First, they differ in their *notional amount*. A company can obtain a few large-sized loans and finance a diverse range of small-sized assets. In Sarah's case from Chapter 1, she might obtain one loan of $60,000 and invest it together with $40,000 of her own savings in her coffee roasting company. Let us assume she buys a coffee roaster for $70,000, a container to store the coffee beans for $6,000, an air dehumidifier for $3,000, and a computer notebook to communicate with customers for $1,000. The rest she keeps in cash for further expenses. Figure 2.3 depicts the balance sheet of Sarah's business.

A company might also own assets that generate profits over decades, but are financed with loans that have a shorter *maturity*. In the above example, Sarah's loan might have a term to maturity of five years. Her coffee roaster, on the other side, might be in operation for more than 10 years.

Asset Side		Liability Side	
20	Cash	Liabilities	60
1	Computer notebook	(e.g., loans taken out)	
6	Container		
3	Air dehumidifier		
70	Coffee roaster		
		Equity	40
100	Total	Total	100

Figure 2.3 *The balance sheet of Sarah's coffee roasting business (in thousands)*

Finally, the *risk profile* of assets and liabilities can differ. Different assets feature different risks. In Sarah's case, the probability that her computer notebook crashes and becomes worthless is higher than that her coffee roaster breaks down. Furthermore, some asset risks are correlated, while others are unrelated. The risk of Sarah's notebook crashing is unrelated to the risk of her container being stolen. However, if her container is stolen, she will also lose the dehumidifier that she installed in it. *Diversification* can be achieved by having assets whose risks are not perfectly correlated with each other.

In addition, the risks of the assets are unevenly distributed among the equity and the different liabilities. If Sarah needs to replace her computer notebook, the cost will eat into her equity. The loan, in contrast, remains unimpaired. In general, shareholders bear more risk than debt holders. In our example, Sarah is the sole owner, or shareholder, of equity in her company and the lenders are the debt holders who granted Sarah a loan.

When assets differ from liabilities in their notional amount, maturity, and risk profile, we speak of *asset transformation*. Asset transformation does not only take place on the balance sheet of Sarah's coffee roasting company, but also on the balance sheets of banks. In contrast to nonfinancial companies, banks hold almost no real assets, such as machinery, but mostly financial assets, such as loans. Banks transform the notional amounts, maturities, and risks of financial assets.

How does asset transformation at banks work? First, a bank transforms the notional size by granting large loans and issuing small deposits. The bank is able to provide larger loans than an individual household ever could. This activity is called *pooling*; the bank pools many small funds from depositors.

Banks transform risks mainly by diversifying and structuring their balance sheets. They *diversify* their loan portfolio: By lending to hundreds of borrowers in different industries, the losses on the overall loan portfolio become less volatile and fairly predictable. Furthermore, the bank owners themselves have some money on the line to absorb losses on on loans—that is, the bank operates with positive equity. In case of any losses on the bank's assets, shareholders suffer losses first, and deposits are less risky than the bank's assets.

Finally, banks transform maturities. While most loans have maturities of several years, banks offer *contractual liquidity*: They promise that their deposits can be withdrawn anytime. Deposits feature a term to maturity of zero. To meet occasional withdrawal requests from depositors, banks hold a *liquidity reserve*—for example, in the form of cash—on the asset side of their balance sheets. Because the liquidity reserve is only a fraction of all deposits, today's banking is also called *fractional reserve banking.*[7]

Recall how the mismatch between borrowers and lenders inhibits credit. Borrowers prefer loans with large principal and long maturity to undertake risky investments. Lenders prefer loans with small principal and short maturity to stay flexible and be exposed to as little credit and liquidity risk as possible. Banks bridge these mismatching preferences with asset transformation.

Indeed, banks are so successful transforming assets that depositors do not care about the issues of credit anymore. Most of us forgot that as depositors, we are ultimately lenders. We lend money to our bank, but we no longer think about the problems of credit. We do not lose sleep over information asymmetries, credit risk, or the fear that we cannot access liquidity. We rarely challenge the bank's promise to exchange our deposit with money anytime on demand. In other words, we call our bank deposits "money."

By convincing us that deposits are as good as money, banks convinced us to participate in credit. Banks enhanced credit availability for businesses and facilitated the development of a capital-intensive economy. This ultimately resulted in huge gains in the economic welfare of society. Quite naturally, however, banking not only enhances credit but also affects money. The increased availability of credit is just one side of the story. The flip side is money creation.

Banking Is Money Creation Out of Credit

What we have explained above is perceived by many as what the business of banks is all about: Banks collect money from depositors and grant loans to borrowers with depositors' money. But this view is incomplete. Banks can grant loans without having received money from a depositor first. They create money by extending credit.

For many people, banks creating money squares with the idea of government having a monopoly on issuing money. Let us be clear that banks do not issue cash; that is, they do not print dollar bills. Only the government is allowed to do so.

At this point, let us elaborate on why the government can actually print dollar bills. Today's money is organized as a *fiat monetary regime*. Fiat money is usually money by law. The government determines its production, declares that taxes and government services have to be paid with it, and settles its own debt with this money. The distinct feature of fiat money is that it has no intrinsic value. The dollar bill in your pocket is useful as money only, and no one promises the exchange into any good or service at a fixed rate. You can buy other goods only at market-determined prices.[8]

Government-issued money is often called *outside money*, because it is created outside the banking system. Besides cash, central bank reserves are also outside money. Central bank reserves are electronic money created by the central bank and held by banks, which use this form of outside money as a medium of exchange—that is, for clearing purposes—in interbank transactions or as a very liquid and safe store of value.

In contrast, *inside money* is created *within* the banking system. Despite not being created by the government but by private institutions, inside money serves the same purpose as outside money. It can be used as a medium of exchange or as a store of value, and it has the same unit of account as outside money.[9]

Deposits are the best-known form of inside money. Most people do not distinguish between cash (outside money) and their deposit account (inside money). They can use both forms of money for making payments in a shop, either by handing over a dollar bill or by paying by check or debit card.

How do banks create inside money? In fact, we have already described it. By transforming assets, banks can offer deposits that are as good as money. Let us look at an example of inside money creation to clarify the idea. For simplicity, assume that there are no banks, and Alex wants to become the first banker in our economy. In order to establish a bank, he obtains a bank license so that he is legally allowed to offer deposits. In addition, he provides $80 in outside money out of his own funds. Hence, his bank is established with an initial balance sheet of $80 cash on the asset side and $80 of equity on the liability side.

The first customer of the bank, Sarah, successfully applies for a $60 loan to buy a coffee roaster. Alex's bank grants the loan by simply expanding the balance sheet: On the asset side, the bank records the loan to Sarah; on the liability side, the bank opens a deposit of $60 in her name. The bank created credit out of nothing; it put two credit contracts of equal size, a deposit and a loan of $60, on both sides of its balance sheet. For simplicity, let us assume that interest on both the loan and the deposit is zero.

Next, Sarah buys a coffee roaster for $60 from Ryan. She could do so by withdrawing the money from her bank deposit. But as Ryan has recently opened a deposit account at Alex's bank, he suggests transferring the money from her to his account. Why does Ryan suggest this? First, Alex's bank does have high liquidity reserves, so he confidently believes in being able to withdraw outside money if he needs to. Second, a large equity buffer makes Ryan confident that he will avoid losses if the bank incurs losses on its assets—for example, if Sarah is not able to pay back her loan. Third, bank payment is more convenient than cash payment.

In turn, Sarah pays for the roaster by writing a check. One trade in the real economy takes place, but no outside money changes hands. Instead, deposits are used, and the bank's balance sheet acts as an accounting system of exchange. The bank transformed the credit that it created out of nothing into inside money.

Figure 2.4 illustrates the different bookings on the bank's balance sheet. In the first step, Sarah obtained a loan from the bank. By extending the loan, the bank expanded its asset side by $60. At the same time, the liability side was expanded by a $60 deposit for Sarah. In the second step, Sarah buys a coffee roaster from Ryan. The $60 goes from Sarah's to Ryan's deposit. The bank deposits are used as a medium of exchange; that is, they are inside money.

The bank will likely grant more loans if it finds trustworthy borrowers. Assume that Julia is such a borrower. She also applies successfully for a loan of $60, and the bank opens a deposit in Julia's name. The balance sheet and the supply of inside money expand further. After the loan has been granted to Julia, the total supply of both inside and outside money has been multiplied by a factor of 2.5 from the initial amount of outside money of $80. Let us assume that Julia opens a coffee shop also and buys another coffee roaster from Ryan. Figure 2.5 illustrates the effects of these events on the bank's balance sheet.

Suppose that the coffee roaster salesperson, Ryan, is a coffee lover and buys freshly roasted coffee from Sarah for $60. Thus, $60 from Ryan's deposit is booked back to the deposit of Sarah. Sarah could use her deposit to buy other things needed for her business. But let us assume that her loan will reach maturity soon, and she has to repay it. When she repays her loan, the bank's balance sheet will shorten. The bank cancels Sarah's outstanding loan with her deposit. In turn, the amount of inside money in the economy decreases. Again, we have illustrated the balance sheet after these events in Figure 2.6.

1. Alex establishes a bank.

Asset Side		Liability Side	
80	Cash		
		Equity Alex	80
80	Total	Total	80

2. Sarah obtains a loan from the bank.

Asset Side		Liability Side	
80	Cash	Deposit Sarah	60
60	Loan Sarah		
		Equity Alex	80
140	Total	Total	140

3. Sarah buys a coffee roaster from Ryan.

Asset Side		Liability Side	
80	Cash	Deposit Sarah	0
60	Loan Sarah	Deposit Ryan	60
		Equity Alex	80
140	Total	Total	140

Figure 2.4 Money creation by traditional banking: part one

In our stylized example, neither the bank nor other agents in the economy would need outside money as a medium of exchange. Bank deposits act as the sole medium of exchange. Using the bank's accounting system of exchange was sufficient to facilitate trade. After Alex provided $80 in outside money to set up his bank, outside money did not play any further role in transactions. Note, however, that both the $80 liquidity reserve and the equity buffer served as a trust device—to address liquidity and credit risk—so that Ryan was willing to accept Sarah's deposit for payment in the first place.

Asset Side		Liability Side	
80	Cash	Deposit Sarah	0
60	Loan Sarah	Deposit Ryan	60
		Equity Alex	80
140	Total	Total	140

4. Julia obtains a loan from the bank.

Asset Side		Liability Side	
80	Cash	Deposit Sarah	0
60	Loan Sarah	Deposit Ryan	60
60	Loan Julia	Deposit Julia	60
		Equity Alex	80
200	Total	Total	200

5. Julia buys a coffee roaster from Ryan.

Asset Side		Liability Side	
80	Cash	Deposit Sarah	0
60	Loan Sarah	Deposit Ryan	120
60	Loan Julia	Deposit Julia	0
		Equity Alex	80
200	Total	Total	200

Figure 2.5 Money creation by traditional banking: part two

With banking having such an important effect on both money and credit, it makes sense to call today's financial system a banking system. In a banking system, money is first and foremost inside money. Banks can and do multiply the initial amount of outside money several times on their balance sheets.[10]

Banks decide on how much inside money—that is, deposits—to create based on their assessment of creditworthy projects in the economy.[11] As more loans are granted, a bank's balance sheet ex-

Asset Side		Liability Side	
80	Cash	Deposit Sarah	0
60	Loan Sarah	Deposit Ryan	120
60	Loan Julia	Deposit Julia	0
		Equity Alex	80
200	Total	Total	200

6. Ryan buys coffee from Sarah.

Asset Side		Liability Side	
80	Cash	Deposit Sarah	60
60	Loan Sarah	Deposit Ryan	60
60	Loan Julia	Deposit Julia	0
		Equity Alex	80
200	Total	Total	200

7. Sarah repays her loan.

Asset Side		Liability Side	
80	Cash	Deposit Sarah	0
0	Loan Sarah	Deposit Ryan	60
60	Loan Julia	Deposit Julia	0
		Equity Alex	80
140	Total	Total	140

Figure 2.6 Money destruction by traditional banking

pands. A bank creates inside money by granting new loans, and it destroys money by not replacing repaid loans with new ones. Banks endogenously determine the overall supply of money in the economy by their extension of credit. While some praise the endogenous money supply in a banking system, money creation out of credit comes with serious side effects.

——————————————————— NOTES ———————————————————

1. See Carruthers and Espeland (1991).

2. A withdrawal transaction from Sittah would only appear once on Bonafides's record as a debit on Sittah's account. In contrast, a withdrawal from a bank deposit would lead to two debits: one on Sittah's deposit and one on the cash reserves of the bank. Note that some transactions are also recorded twice with single-entry bookkeeping. For example, the transaction between Sittah and Nathan was recorded twice in the records of Bonafides, once as a debit on Sittah's account and once as a credit on Nathan's account.

3. See Carruthers and Espeland (1991), who elaborate on how double-entry bookkeeping changed the economic thinking of merchants and other businesspeople. Double-entry bookkeeping shaped rational decision making and fostered economic rationalism.

4. Usually, a balance sheet is compiled at the end of every business year. Modern double-entry bookkeeping also includes other financial statements—such as income and cash-flow statements—that report financial activities of a company over time. For our purpose, these accounting statements are of a minor relevance.

5. Public companies finance themselves with equity that is traded on stock exchanges. In this case, the *market value* of the traded equity can deviate from the book value. If not mentioned otherwise, we always refer to the book value when speaking of the value of equity.

6. Technical insolvency is sometimes also referred to as *balance-sheet insolvency*.

7. While banks promise withdrawals at par to all depositors at all times, they are only able to meet a small fraction of withdrawals at any given time. This is why some economists from the Austrian School label the deposit contract as fraud; see, for example, Huerta de Soto and Stroup (2009).

8. The name for this monetary regime is derived from the Latin verb *fiat*, which can be translated as "let there be." It refers to the artificial nature of this money. This sets fiat money apart from some earlier monetary regimes. Historically, societies have often used a scarce commodity as money. Such a monetary regime is called commodity money. Gold and silver coins are probably the best known forms. One might object that gold derives much of its value because it is perceived as money. However, note that gold (and silver, in particular) have some use in the production of goods—something that you cannot say of the dollar bills in your pocket. Similar to commodity money is representative money. It promises the bearer a conversion into a commodity—for example, gold—at a predetermined rate. For a theoretical analysis on why fiat money attains a positive value, see Lagos (2010).

9. Inside money is always created by private banking institutions. Hence, one could call it private inside money. One should not confuse private inside money with private outside money. Private outside money is a private monetary regime that has not been established by a governmental authority. Bitcoin is an example of private outside money. Private inside money, on the other hand, arises as a result of banking within a

given monetary regime. Dollar-denominated deposits are an example of private inside money. Private inside and private outside money can be differentiated by looking at the unit of account. While private outside money creates a new unit of account, private inside money is linked to an existing unit of account; it is denominated in the same unit as the outside money it refers to. Hence, banking is not limited to a governmental monetary regime (public outside money). It is possible that private inside money is created within a private monetary regime (private outside money)— for example, Bitcoin-denominated deposits.

10. For an accessible and topical text on money creation by banks, see McLeay, Radia, and Thomas (2014).

11. Banks are also limited by banking regulation. They cannot create unlimited amounts of inside money but usually have to meet two requirements. First, the Federal Reserve System (the Fed) requires that banks hold a certain fraction of issued deposits in the form of outside money. Reserve requirements constrain inside money creation on the asset side of a bank's balance sheet. Second, banks are also subject to minimum equity capital requirements (henceforth, capital requirements). These requirements oblige a bank to maintain a minimum equity-to-asset ratio and restrict inside money creation on the liability side. While reserve requirements are imposed to guarantee liquidity of a bank, capital requirements are intended, among other things, to ensure solvency of a bank. We come back to banking regulation in the next chapter.

3 The Problems with Banking

Banking seems to be magic, as it manages to reconcile two mutually exclusive financial relationships. On the asset side of their balance sheets, banks grant loans that borrowers have to repay only after several years. On the liability side, banks promise depositors that their deposits can be withdrawn at any time. By transforming credit into money, bankers appear to have found the philosopher's stone. Unfortunately, banking comes at a heavy price.

The Bank Run Is the Achilles' Heel of Banking

The biggest strength of something often guides one to its biggest weakness. While banking manages to match borrowers and lenders, it does so at the cost of liquidity risk. Banks extend long-term loans and issue inside money, thereby raising the possibility that they might not be able to serve depositors' withdrawals. Liquidity risk makes banking fragile.

Most of the time, liquidity risk does not materialize. As we have mentioned, banks hold liquidity reserves in the form of outside money to meet occasional withdrawals of depositors. On ordinary days, banks' reserves are sufficient. In times of distress, however, banks might find themselves in a situation where they have to fully deplete their liquidity reserves to meet depositors' withdrawals. If this happens, banks are said to be illiquid.

The most prominent situation that leads to the illiquidity of banks is the bank run. A *bank run* is a situation where many depositors want to withdraw money at the same time. Banks can only service a certain number of withdrawals within a given time period. The threshold is determined by the amount of liquidity reserves available. If depositors withdraw more, banks become illiquid.

When a bank has no liquidity reserves left, it needs to sell other assets such as long-term loans it has granted in the past. Selling long-term loans is difficult. Potential buyers do not know much about the quality of the loans. The uncertainty will induce buyers to buy bank loans only at a discount. Banks are thus forced to sell their loans at a loss. Consequently, a bank is never able to raise enough outside money to meet the withdrawal demands of all of its depositors at once. If too many depositors withdraw their money, banks collapse. This fragility is the flip side of banking.

Depositors "run" banks because only the first ones who withdraw their money are successful in doing so. Someone who is arriving too late at the cashier risks losing the deposited money. If depositors hear rumors about their bank being in trouble, they are well advised to run and withdraw their money. Should it turn out that the rumors were wrong, they can still put their money back on their account. But if the initial rumors prove to be correct, they have managed to save their deposited money.

Even initially unfounded rumors can trigger bank runs and become self-fulfilling, as it is in the very nature of banks that they can never serve all depositors. Depositors do not necessarily run a bank because it is poorly managed, or because it suffers losses. Even a perfectly operated bank can experience a bank run. It is the fundamental weakness of banking.[1]

Bank runs are a constant threat for banks and have been a frequent phenomenon throughout the history of banking. Many people in advanced economies, however, had forgotten about bank runs—until September 2007, when it happened again. The British bank Northern Rock suffered a run by its depositors.[2]

You might think, what is the fuss with bank runs? It is just some depositors losing money that they lent to a bank. Usually, when a nonbanking company goes bankrupt and its lenders lose money, the overall economy does not suffer. In the end, business failure is the consequence of a market economy where everyone can enter the market freely.

But banking is not just a business model; it is the creation of money out of credit. Due to their self-fulfilling nature, bank runs tend to be contagious. If bank runs occur simultaneously at different banks, we speak of a *banking panic*.

In a banking panic, people lose trust in the banking system. Depositors withdraw their deposits from various banks, even from the healthy ones. As was just discussed, this will lead to the illiquidity of the respective banks even if they are well managed. The result is widespread bank failure. Such a banking panic occurred in the years between 1929 and 1933, when about 9,000 banks suspended operations.[3]

In a banking panic, the aggregate amount of credit plummets. Banks that went bankrupt can no longer grant loans. Banks still in business stop lending money to both other banks and businesses, so that they will have sufficient reserves to meet withdrawals of panicking depositors. The banking system is not able to finance the same amount of credit as it did before the panic. This effect is usually referred to as *credit crunch*: Companies losing access to credit during a banking panic can no longer fund their operations and thus go bankrupt. Production stalls, people employed in these companies lose their jobs, and the government's tax receipts fall.

Moreover, as banks create inside money, bank failures affect the price level. The deposits of insolvent or illiquid banks cease being money. As we have seen, banks still in business stop rolling over loans and increase their reserves; they destroy inside money. Less money is available in the economy, and prices start to fall. The monetary phenomenon of falling prices is called *deflation*. In the case of a banking panic, deflation is a distortion of prices induced by a particular organizational feature of the financial system—the creation of money out of credit. Falling prices further depress economic activity in the real economy, and a vicious circle of credit and money destruction picks up the pace.[4]

A single bank run can thus trigger a chain reaction that ultimately undermines the functioning of the financial system. It first affects other banks, then the overall supply of both money and credit in the economy. In the worst case, a banking panic can lead to a complete meltdown of the financial system, pushing the economy into a deflationary spiral and a severe recession. It is the pivotal role of banking in our financial system that makes bank runs so disastrous. Bank runs are the Achilles' heel of banking.

Government Guarantees Can Prevent Bank Runs...

Bank runs are inherent to every banking system. They have been analyzed in economic theory and were frequently experienced in practice.[5] It is no surprise that people started to think about ways to prevent them a long time ago. The most common instruments to prevent bank runs are deposit insurance and lender-of-last-resort policies.

Deposit Insurance

As the term suggests, deposit insurance insures the money held by depositors at banks. The government or a collective of banks guarantees all deposits, usually up to a certain amount.[6] Credible insurance eliminates the incentive for depositors to run a bank, despite rumors about a potential bank failure. The insured depositor will not lose any money even if such rumors turn out to be correct and the bank ultimately fails. Hence, the mere announcement of credible deposit insurance can prevent bank runs.[7]

This is an attractive feature that explains the rapid spread of the concept. Deposit insurance was first introduced in the United States as a reaction to the Great Depression in the 1930s.[8] Since then, many countries have introduced some sort of deposit insurance.[9]

Central Banks as Lenders of Last Resort

Central banks were established earlier than deposit insurance. In the United States, for instance, the *Federal Reserve System*—better known as *the Fed*—was established in 1912 as a reaction to a severe banking panic in 1907.[10] Central banks not only act as lenders of last resort, but also conduct monetary policy. They manage the *money supply*, which is the the total amount of outside and inside money in the economy. Understanding how central banks do this is important to understand their role during bank runs and banking panics.

Let us briefly discuss how the Fed conducts monetary policy in the United States during normal times, that is, in absence of any bank runs or banking panics.[11] Recall that today's monetary system is built on fiat money, which has no intrinsic value. You might think that the Fed simply prints money and then spends it. That is not exactly what happens. The Fed does not walk down Main Street to go on a shopping spree. Rather, it walks down Wall Street to go on a lending spree. Monetary policy always involves banks.

Open market operations are the most important tool the Fed has to affect the money supply. Open market operations can involve the outright sale or purchase of financial assets from banks. If the Fed buys financial assets such as government bonds, it increases the amount of outside money in the economy. Open market operations can also be conducted by engaging in repurchase agreements (henceforth *repos*) with banks. A repo is similar to a short-term collateralized loan. If the Fed lends money via repos, it also increases the amount of outside money in the economy.[12]

Spending money the central banker's way tends to be profitable. If the Fed lends money via a repo, it usually earns interest. The same is true for holding financial assets it acquired as a result of its open market operations. The profits from money creation are called *seignorage*. Most of it goes to the government, that is, the U.S. Treasury.[13]

The ultimate goal of central banks is not, however, to make a profit. Seignorage can be considered a by-product of monetary policy. The central banks' mandate is to preserve price stability and to promote employment.

As we have seen, banking panics result in devastating effects on both the price system and employment. Acting as a lender of last resorts thus fits into central banks' mandate. Central banks acting as *lenders of last resort* lend directly to struggling banks during banking panics. These banks can then service the withdrawals of their depositors. As such, central banks can contain banking panics and restore confidence in the banking system. The Fed, for instance, can support struggling banks during banking panics and has done so repeatedly during its history.[14]

... But at the Cost of Moral Hazard

It appears that we have found a way to safeguard banking and prevent banking panics. Both deposit insurance and lender-of-last-resort policies tackle the self-fulfilling-prophecy character of bank runs. They do so by taking away the fear of depositors to lose money.

Relieving depositors of their fear alters their behavior. Most of us are actually depositors, so you might ask: What change of behavior? We actually have not realized this change in behavior, as it has happened over almost a century. While people living in the first half of the 20th century were well aware that bank deposits carry some risks, later generations have grown up with the belief that bank deposits are absolutely safe. We have to distinguish between normal and crisis times here. Bank deposits have been perceived as rather safe during normal times ever since. Today, however, we also perceive them as riskless in times of crises because of deposit insurance and central banking.

Most people do not feel a difference between holding cash and depositing money at a bank. As a result, risk is not an issue when opening a bank deposit. For most of us, fees, interest rates, and the location of the bank's branches are decisive when determining our bank of choice. Risk is, if at all, only a minor concern.[15]

The change in depositors' behavior is the result of both deposit insurance and lender-of-last-resort facilities, and it has far-reaching consequences. Knowing that depositors do not care about banks' risk profiles, banks take more risk in their investment decisions. Hence, the powerful medicine to prevent banking panics comes with the side effect of moral hazard in the form of excessive risk taking.[16]

To understand why banks take excessive risk, we need to discuss limited liability, a concept from corporate law. The term *limited liability* is self-explanatory: The owners of limited liability companies are liable only up to a certain amount—usually their initial investment—for outstanding liabilities of that company. Limited liability is justified because it fosters entrepreneurship and eases the financing for large industrial projects. Today, most banks—in particular, the large ones—are set up as limited liability companies.

While limited liability offers advantages, it also changes the incentives of company owners. Since losses are limited but profits are not, it is a framework that can encourage *excessive risk taking*. The owner of a limited liability company can be induced to take on more risk than is socially optimal. An example illustrates the idea of excessive risk taking. Let us assume you can choose between two projects with different risk and return profiles:

Project One: The return is 10% for sure. You end up with 110% of the amount invested. The expected return of this project is 10%.

Project Two: Returns are uncertain, either +60% or −60%. You either end up with 160% or 40% of the amount invested with equal probabilities. As a result, the expected return of this project is 0%.

Having the choice between these two projects, you would be well advised to choose Project One because it yields a better expected return than Project Two. If you are not operating within a limited liability company, your expected profit is equal to the expected return of the projects. Having $2 in hand, for instance, you would invest them in Project One.

Now imagine you set up a limited liability company with your $2 and borrow $8. On the asset side of your company's balance sheet, you have $10 in cash. On the liability side, you have $8 debt and $2 equity. For simplicity, let us assume that the interest on your debt is zero.

You are now the owner of this company, and you have to choose again between Project One and Project Two. Your liability is limited to the equity you put up initially; that is, your loss in the bad state is capped at $2.

If you choose Project One, you make a sure profit of $1. What happens if you chose Project Two? If things go bad, you lose your equity, hence your payoff is minus $2. You can pass on the other $4 losses to your lenders. In the best case scenario, however, you make a profit of $6. As a result, the expected profit for you as the equity holder is $2. You prefer Project Two over Project One, even though its overall expected return is worse. Operating within a limited liability company, your expected profit can differ from the expected returns of the projects.

The owners of a limited liability company do not carry the full downside risk of their decisions. They can take excessive risks at the expense of their lenders. Lenders take some of the loss in the case of a bad outcome, while their return if things turn out well is capped by the preset interest payment.

To discourage the owners of a firm from taking excessive risks, lenders want them to have enough "skin in the game." The skin usually takes the form of equity. As long as the ratio of equity to total assets (henceforth, *equity ratio*) is high enough, owners have much at stake and will refrain from taking excessive risks. In the above example, as the owner, you would avoid excessive risk and choose Project One if the equity ratio was above 40%—that is, if your equity was greater than $4.

Understandably, lenders have to look closely the equity ratio— the ratio of equity to total assets—of their borrowers. In a banking system, banks are prominent lenders and grant loans to companies. Banks are well aware that their borrowers might take excessive risks due to limited liability. This is why they tighten their lending if an individual or a company features a too low equity ratio, in which case the borrower is said to be too indebted. Excessive risk taking is part of the moral hazard issues arising with credit, as discussed above. Banks solve this by adequately monitoring companies (among other actions). Furthermore, they can include covenants in their loan contracts that require lenders to put up collateral. If borrowers lose their collateral when things turn out bad, they will be less likely to take excessive risks.[17] In the end, while no one is legally in charge of preventing excessive risk taking arising from limited liability, lenders in general and banks in particular watch borrowers carefully.

As banks themselves have a capital structure consisting of debt and equity, the classic problem of "who watches the watchmen" arises. Obviously, banks should be restrained from lowering their equity ratio too much by their lenders, that is, by the depositors. But with government guarantees in place, depositors know that their money is safe no matter what. They have no incentive to step in if their bank takes excessive risks. Knowing this, banks indeed take excessive risks.[18]

Moral Hazard Calls for Banking Regulation

Governments are again in demand. They have to implement measures that curb excessive risk taking. Governments have resorted to different measures. We subsume all measures trying to get a grip on moral hazard by banks—such as excessive risk taking—under the term *banking regulation*. At first sight, one might think that requiring banks to adhere to a simple equity ratio would be enough to deal with moral hazard. As we will see below, it is not that simple, which is why early banking regulation focused more on other measures.

Early Banking Regulation

In the United States, both the Fed and the Federal Deposit Insurance Corporation (FDIC) play an important role in the supervision of banks. The FDIC is the governmental agency in charge of managing deposit insurance. It makes sure that depositors get their money back if a bank fails. Of course, the people at both the Fed and the FDIC have been aware that banks' risk appetite increases with deposit insurance. Hence, they closely observe insured banks.[19]

The FDIC commenced operations when deposit insurance was introduced during the Great Depression. It closely supervised banks and imposed tight regulations to restrict the range of business activities that insured banks were allowed to engage in.[20] The restrictions were remarkably successful. After World War II, the risk taking of banks seemed to be under control. Banking was tightly regulated and boring, but also stable.[21]

The calm was, however, deceptive. Since the establishment of the Fed, the equity ratios of U.S. banks have shown a continuous downward trend. Going further back in time, you can see that bank equity ratios have fallen from above 30% in the 1870s to about 5% in the 1970s.[22]

With such low equity levels, excessive risk taking is attractive. And indeed, banks started to change their behavior in the 1970s; they began to take more risks.[23] But excessive risk taking was not the only thing that gave regulators headaches. They also faced a banking industry that had become increasingly globalized.[24]

Modern Banking Regulation: The Basel Capital Accord

Regulators relied upon a national framework for banking regulation until the 1980s. The failure of the German Bank Herstatt in 1974, which led to large losses at non-German banks, sparked the political initiative to tackle ever-decreasing equity levels of banks at an international level.[25] Banking regulation had to follow the trend of banking and become globalized as well.[26] The G10 countries set up the Basel Committee on Banking Supervision to deal with globalized banking.

The committee established the Basel Capital Accord, an international framework for capital requirements better known as Basel I.[27] *Capital requirements* require banks to adhere to a certain equity ratio. While they could just as well be called "equity requirements," it is common usage to call the equity of banks "capital."[28]

As we have mentioned, one could think, at first sight, that implementing capital requirements is not that difficult. It seems that regulators only have to agree on a sufficiently high equity ratio and oblige banks to adhere to this figure. Unfortunately, introducing explicit capital requirements that get a grip on excessive risk taking is no simple task at all.

To be effective, capital requirements need to consider the risk-iness of banks' assets. To see that a one-size-fits-all capital requirement is inadequate, one simply has to consider how banks behave as lenders. When banks decide whether a borrower is trustworthy and financially sound, they consider not only the equity ratio but other factors as well—for example, in which industry the borrower is active. In addition, banks often specify covenants in loan contracts that go beyond a simple capital requirement. Covenants can ban, for example, the use of loans for speculative investments on stock markets. When granting loans, banks do not stipulate a simple equity ratio.

Similarly, capital requirements for banks that merely require a particular equity ratio are too simplistic. They fail to account for the risk dimension of the assets a bank holds. Remember the example of excessive risk taking above. If you were required to meet a 40% equity ratio, as in that example, you would refrain from taking excessive risks. Suppose, however, you could select yet another project called Project Three, which comes with returns of +100% or −100%. Given this additional choice, a 40% equity ratio would no longer be sufficient. Now, the minimum equity ratio has to be set at least at 80% to discourage you from taking excessive risks.[29]

The designers of Basel I dealt with this difficulty by introducing the concept of risk weights. *Risk-weighted capital requirements* mean that you have to put up more equity if you hold riskier assets. So in our example, banks should be required to hold more equity if they chose Project Three than Project Two. And if they chose Project One, the capital requirement could be even lower.[30]

Risk-weighted capital requirements are quite involved banking regulations. The real world offers more than three projects with well-defined payoffs. A bank can invest in millions of different assets. It is very difficult for the regulator to apply reasonable risk weights on all these assets. Implementing internationally co-ordinated, risk-weighted capital requirements is by no means an easy task.[31]

Unfortunately, the efforts of the regulators did not pay off. Basel I did not herald the return of a stable banking period. The frequency and severity of financial crises continued to increase.[32] Something happened that undermined the efforts of regulators: the digital revolution.

───────────────────────── NOTES ─────────────────────────

1. For analytical models, refer to Bryant (1980) and Diamond and Dybvig (1983), who have both studied the basic mechanisms of bank runs. A different interpretation of bank runs is given by Calomiris and Kahn (1991), who interpret bank runs as a way for depositors to force liquidation if the bank acts against their interests.

2. See Shin (2009). While this bank run was visible, we see in Chapter 6 that the more significant banking panic during the financial crisis of 2007–08 happened in the shadows.

3. Federal Deposit Insurance Corporation (1984, 3).

4. See Fisher (1933a) for a theory of debt deflation. For an accessible account on the perils of deflation, see Bernanke (2002).

5. For an overview of bank runs and banking panics in economic history and theory, see Gorton and Winton (2003, sec. 4). For an overview of the economic history of financial crisis, see, for example, Reinhart and Rogoff (2009b), Kindleberger (1993), and Kindleberger and Aliber (2005).

6. In deposit insurance schemes, the amount insured is often capped. The main reason is that moral hazard issues arising from deposit insurance would worsen if the insurance was all-encompassing. We discuss moral hazard issues in the next chapter. For an extensive discussion of deposit insurance, see Demirgüç-Kunt and Kane (2002).

7. Silber (2009) argues that deposit insurance, implemented by the Emergency Banking Act of 1933, was the turnaround action that stopped the banking panic during the Great Depression.

8. See Federal Deposit Insurance Corporation (2010). The Great Depression was a severe and global economic recession. The fall in U.S. stock prices at the end of the "roaring" 1920s marked its beginning. The Great Depression lasted for over a decade, and the economies around the world did not fully recover until the advent of World War II.

9. See Demirgüç-Kunt, Kane, and Laeven (2008) for a comprehensive overview.

10. Already back in the 19th century, Bagehot (1873) was a prominent advocate of lender-of-last-resort policy. For an overview on the early history of the Fed, see Johnson (2010).

11. Changes in monetary policy during the financial crisis of 2007–08 will be discussed later. Note that in what follows, we do not discuss the detailed mechanics behind monetary policy—that is, setting the federal funds rate, the market for federal funds, changing reserve requirements, and so forth. A thorough discussion of the monetary

policy in the United States can be found in Board of Governors of the Federal Reserve System (2005).

12. We discuss features of repos in greater detail in Chapter 5. Note that the Fed used to only buy and sell government securities, that is, U.S. Treasury securities. For repos, other securities are also accepted as collateral. In the aftermath of the financial crisis of 2007–08, this rule has been relaxed (see Chapter 6).

13. As the Fed used to hold only government bonds, this seems to be a bit of an odd exercise. Both the Fed and the U.S. Treasury are government bodies. Holding government bonds, the Fed earns interest, that is, seignorage. This interest is paid by the U.S. Treasury. But in the end, the seignorage gains of the Fed mostly flow back to the U.S. Treasury. In a way, the Treasury is buying—at least partly—goods and services with newly issued outside money. The channel is obscured by the central bank buying government bonds on the secondary market. Hence, some money goes from the Fed to Wall Street to the Treasury and, finally, to Main Street.

14. Section 13(3) of the Federal Reserve Act allows the Board of Governors of the Federal Reserve System to implement a wide range of measures to help financial institutions that face liquidity issues (see Fettig 2002, 2008).

15. As a point in case, less than 4% of the participants in the Survey of Consumer Finances (SCF) have considered "safety and absence of risk" the most important reason for choosing an institution for their main checking account in 2010 (Bricker et al. 2012, 33).

16. While deposit insurance always leads to moral hazard, a strict application of Bagehot's principle for lenders of last resort to only lend to solvent but illiquid banks should not lead to moral hazard. However, the Fed repeatedly lent to institutions that had also solvency issues; see, for example, Schwartz (1992). Furthermore, it is difficult to differentiate between liquidity and solvency issues in a banking panic.

17. In this regard, putting up collateral is similar to putting up more equity.

18. See Kareken and Wallace (1978) for an early analysis of how deposit insurance induces banks to take more risks. Grossman (1992) shows empirically that thrifts in the 1930s that were lightly regulated but insured gradually took on more risk than their uninsured counterparts. Gropp, Gruendl, and Guettler (2014) analyzed the behavior of German saving banks after their government guarantees were removed. It turned out that these banks significantly reduced risk taking.

19. See Buser, Chen, and Kane (1981) for how the provision of deposit insurance is conceptually linked to bank supervision.

20. The Glass-Steagall Act and the Bank Holding Company Act put tight portfolio restrictions on insured banks and functionally separated banks from other financial companies such as broker-dealers or insurance companies; see Benston (1994) and Bhattacharya, Boot, and Thakor (1998).

21. Banking after the Great Depression was sometimes described as the 3-6-3 model. Bankers borrowed money at 3%, lent it out at 6%, and were off to the golf courts at 3 pm. For a discussion, see Walter (2006).

22. Hanson, Kashyap, and Stein (2011, 19).

23. The Federal Deposit Insurance Corporation (1984) describes the behavioral change starting in the 1960s: "The new generation of bankers who came to power in the 1960s abandoned the traditional conservatism that had characterized the industry for many years. Instead, they began to strive for more rapid growth in assets, deposits and income. The trend toward aggressiveness and risk taking was particularly pronounced among large banks" (p. 7).

24. See Aliber (1984) for an overview. He notes that after the first wave of banking globalization in the years prior to World War I, a second wave started in the 1960s.

25. See Basel Committee on Banking Supervision (2009).

26. See Kapstein (1989) for a detailed discussion of the international aspect of capital requirements. The difficulty of dealing with the international dimension of capital requirements has become clear again after the financial crisis of 2007–08. Numerous countries tried to tighten up capital requirements without international coordination. The affected banks in turn argued that they were disadvantaged, and some of them even threatened openly to move business to another jurisdiction. The CEO of J.P. Morgan, for example, described the implementation of stricter capital requirements as "Anti-American" (Braithwaite & Jenkins, 2011).

27. For the original document, see Basel Committee on Banking Supervision (1988).

28. For a critical discussion of this peculiarity, see Admati and Hellwig (2013).

29. With a total equity of $8 and debt of $2, investing $10 in Project Three yields $10 in the good state and −$8 in the bad state, which equals an expected return of $1. This is the same return as Project One would yield. Note that banks' equity ratios are actually much lower than in our example. They have been as low as 3%. What would you do if you were a bank, and you could choose either playing roulette or buying Treasury bills with 97% borrowed money? You would be a fool if you did not play roulette. Imagine you borrowed $97 and invested $3 of your own funds. For the sake of clarity, we assume again that you were able to borrow the money at zero interest (something that is accurate to assume for large banks these days). If your risky investment strategy was betting on one color in roulette, you would either gain $100 or lose $3 with equal probability. Unless you were extremely risk averse, you would never buy the Treasury bill in this situation. Of course, we do not say that banks lend money and take a trip to Las Vegas. These examples are for illustration only. In Chapter 7, we discuss current strategies of banks to take on risks.

30. Kim and Santomero (1988) demonstrate the need for risk-weighted capital requirements to prevent banks from excessive risk taking.

31. For a further discussion of issues arising, see, for example, Jackson et al. (1999) and D. Jones (2000). Political considerations also shape capital requirements. Basel I, for instance, treated some government debt as risk-free. Thus, banks were not required to put up equity against holding particular government bonds. These government bonds became more attractive for banks, and banks started to hold more of them. See Haubrich and Wachtel (1993) for empirical evidence. Starting in 2010, the

European sovereign debt crisis has forcefully demonstrated that the zero-risk weight for some government debt was flawed. Banks struggled to absorb the losses on some of their government debt holdings. The preferential treatment of government bonds in contemporary banking regulation has created a strong tie between governments and banks: Banks finance governments, and governments guarantee the liabilities of banks. We come back to this point in Part Three.

32. See, for example, Figure 10.1 in Reinhart and Rogoff (2009b) and Minsky (1986).

PART TWO

Banking in the Digital Age

$\underline{4}$ Banking Is Not Limited to Banks

We started Part One by demonstrating the need for banking in the industrial age. Banking matches borrowers with lenders and, hence, allows credit to flourish. Explaining the mechanics of traditional banking, we found out that banks match borrowers with lenders by creating inside money in the form of deposits. We then turned to the problems arising with traditional banking and discussed the various measures taken to get these problems under control.

So far, calling for the end of banking seems unfounded. Banking supports a capital-intensive economy, government guarantees prevent banking panics, and banking regulation can deal with the undesired side effects of guarantees. Indeed, banking was a sensible way to organize the financial system in the industrial age.

The tables are turning with modern information technology entering the stage. Part Two of this book is about how the digital revolution disrupted the delicate balance among banking, government guarantees, and banking regulation, and how banking eventually got out of control. What to do given the state of banking in the digital age will be discussed in Part Three.

Recall the mechanics of traditional banking. Banks grant loans and create deposits. All transactions are recorded on a single balance sheet. The key elements are loans, liquidity reserves, deposits, and equity. One balance sheet is sufficient to operate traditional banking. Apart from the knowledge of double-entry bookkeeping, you only need paper and pen.

In the industrial age, banks were reluctant to complicate their business model. Financial relationships had to be recorded and reconciled on paper. Every transaction had to be confirmed with the counterparty using telephone calls and physical letters. Moving a credit contract from one balance sheet to another one was costly; it required manual effort and generated a lot of paperwork. Credit was immobile in the industrial age, and banks voluntarily operated in a simple and confined setup.

Given that the technology available in the industrial age largely limited banking to bank balance sheets, governments could get a grip on the problems of banking. On the one hand, governments guaranteed deposits such that banks no longer had to fear bank runs. On the other hand, governments tightly regulated everything that happened on the bank balance sheet. They could effectively prevent banks from abusing the guarantees by taking excessive risks.

The Digital Revolution and the Rise of Shadow Banking

In the 1970s, information technology emerged and marked the beginning of the digital revolution. Computers replaced typewriters, and information transmission migrated from analog to digital channels. In turn, financial institutions started to record credit on electronic accounts and manage payments on electronic systems. They also automated their back-office operations and began to support their trading activities with electronic tools. Banks were now able to handle more complex and dynamic financial structures with multiple balance-sheet layers. The digital revolution mobilized credit.[1]

The advent of the digital revolution meant that banking was no longer confined to the traditional way of recording and managing money and credit. Information technology supports many more options than simply holding loans on a balance sheet until maturity. Banks could now slice, dice, and redistribute credit over a chain of balance sheets at negligible costs.

And they made heavy use of the new opportunities. The start of the digital revolution was followed by the rise of shadow banking. The term *shadow banking* is used inconsistently to describe a variety of financial institutions and networks. We use the term exclusively for the creation of money out of credit outside the traditional banking sector.[2] The first word, *shadow*, refers to banking that is performed out of the banking regulators' spotlight, in the shadows. Figure 4.1 plots the volume of the liabilities of traditional and shadow banking between the 1950s and 2010. Before 1970, shadow banking was virtually inexistent. At the outset of the financial crisis of 2007–08, shadow banking was more important than traditional banking.

The digital revolution explains why shadow banking is possible. But it does not explain why shadow banking was so attractive that

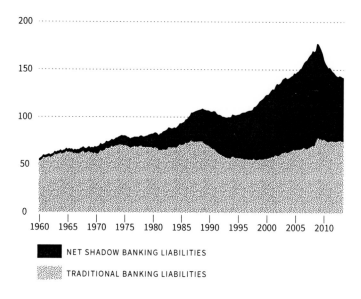

Figure 4.1 *The liabilities of banks and of shadow banking institutions over time in percentage of GDP*

Source: Adrian, Covitz, and Nellie (2014) and Federal Reserve Flow of Funds. Note that as shadow banking is performed over different balance sheets, the figure should be taken as an approximation of shadow banking's true size only. For a discussion of the data used, see Pozsar et al. (2010, 7–9).

it eventually surpassed the traditional banking model within three decades. In the end, banks sticking to their traditional business model should have also benefited from replacing their typewriters with computers. What explains the dramatic rise of shadow banking?

The Boundary Problem of Financial Regulation

Shadow banking's origins in the 1970s hint at the motivation to migrate banking activities into the shadows. Back then, traditional banks were regulated by an interest rate ceiling called *Regulation Q*. The regulator capped the interest rate that banks could offer on their deposits. It was an inconvenient regulation for banks, as it inhibited them from attracting customer deposits, especially in periods of high inflation.

At that time, a new form of financial institution emerged that offered something very similar to bank deposits: *Money market mutual funds (MMMFs)*. They issue deposit-like contracts on the liability side and hold credit contracts with low risk and short maturities on the asset side of their balance sheets. Since MMMFs did not issue deposits in a legal sense, they were not considered to be banks. In turn, they were not subject to the interest rate ceiling and could offer higher returns than banks.[3]

MMMFs were an attractive alternative to banks because they were not subject to banking regulation. But MMMFs are just one part of shadow banking. In the 1970s, new financial institutions emerged that together conducted banking—created money out of credit—without being subject to banking regulation. At the same time, shadow banking allowed banks to circumvent banking regulation.

Capital requirements à la Basel I failed because they regulated banks and not banking. Banks transferred assets to remote balance sheets, while still keeping the economic risk. Banks constructed the relationships to their remote balance sheets such that capital requirements did not apply to assets held there. Consequently, banks could circumvent capital requirements and increase their risk taking without putting more skin in the game. This behavior is called regulatory capital arbitrage.[4]

A working paper of the Basel Committee on Banking Supervision published in 1999 explained that "the volume of regulatory capital arbitrage is large and growing rapidly, especially among the largest banks ... [T]here are indications that in many cases the effect [of securitizations] is to increase a bank's apparent capital ratio relative to the riskiness of its actual book."[5] In other words, to evade capital requirements, banks made sure that risks seemingly disappeared from their balance sheets. The paper concludes that "over time the banks have learnt how to exploit the broad brush nature of the requirements ... For some banks, this has probably started to undermine the meaningfulness of the requirements."[6] The quoted working paper makes clear that even the designers of Basel I were well aware that their efforts to regulate banking failed.

The ability of banks to circumvent restrictions constitutes the *boundary problem of financial regulation*.[7] The boundary problem is a concept that applies to every regulated industry. Whenever a company is required to meet certain regulatory restrictions that are costly, it might be tempted to circumvent the restrictions.

The owners of a chemical company, for instance, might not like costly environmental regulations that eat into their profits. They will search for ways to circumvent regulations, as banks do. Circumventing regulations in the real economy, however, is costly, because companies are dealing with physical objects. A chemical company will probably have to shut down its factory and rebuild it again somewhere else to circumvent undesired regulation.

Physical impediments to circumvent regulation apply to a much lesser extent to banking. Banking happens within the financial system, which is virtual. Banking outside banks—and the boundary problem of financial regulation—has always existed.[8] Before the rise of information technology, however, banks still faced technical obstacles when moving their business elsewhere. Moving financial contracts across balance sheets was costly, as it required manual effort.

The digital revolution has removed these obstacles. With information technology at hand, financial contracts can be moved from one entity to another with only a few mouse clicks or finger taps. Banks can quickly adapt their balance sheet structure and transfer financial assets across balance sheets. Information technology has offered banks a broad range of tools to substitute regulated banking activities with unregulated activities that serve the same economic purpose.[9]

The Financial Techniques of Banking

To make sense of the financial crisis of 2007–08, one needs to have a basic understanding of the mechanics of shadow banking. For this, we have to generalize our understanding of banking beyond that of traditional banking.

Recall that traditional banking is the creation of inside money in the form of bank deposits. When we discussed traditional banking, we noted the three characteristics of how bank deposits constitute inside money. First, bank deposits feature the same divisibility as outside money; that is, they have the same denomination as cash. Second, bank deposits are perceived as risk-free. Third, bank deposits are as liquid as outside money.

The characteristics of bank deposits indicate what is required to perform banking in general. If credit is transformed such that it features the three characteristics of bank deposits described above, it becomes inside money. The three characteristics determine whether a financial asset is inside money. The label of the financial asset is irrelevant. Whether we call inside money "deposits," "MMMF shares," or something else does not matter. If a financial asset is perceived as risk-free, divisible, and liquid as outside money, it is inside money. Correspondingly, we distinguish three types of transformations needed to perform banking: the transformations of notional amount, credit risk, and maturity.[10]

The Transformation of Notional Amount by Pooling

Notional amount is transformed by pooling. *Pooling* happens when assets with large notional amounts are funded by liabilities with small notional amounts. Banking institutions hold financial assets of large notional amounts on the asset side, and they issue financial claims of small notional amounts on the liability side. In the case of traditional banking, for instance, banks hold loans on the asset side and deposits on the liability side of their balance sheets.

The Transformation of Credit Risk by ...

Before we discuss how risk can be transformed, note that monitoring, which we discussed in Part One, does not transform but instead mitigates credit risk. Recall that credit risk arises from the possibility that a borrower cannot pay back a loan (partially or fully). It is driven by the likelihood that a borrower defaults and by the financial loss for the lender if the borrower defaults. By monitoring, one can lower aggregate risk in the economy but never fully eliminate it; credit always involves time and uncertainty and, thus, credit risk.

In contrast to monitoring, credit risk transformation techniques do not change aggregate credit risk, but they redistribute existing credit risk.[11] Financial institutions use them to distribute risk among different stakeholders. In essence, banking shifts credit risk away from the liabilities that eventually become inside money. Let us look at the four different techniques for credit-risk transformation in detail.

Diversification, ...

Diversification is an elementary financial technique. While pooling and diversification are conceptually different, pooling often is a prerequisite for lenders to diversify credit risk.[12] Financial institutions diversify their assets, for example, by granting loans to various borrowers so that credit losses on the overall portfolio become less extreme and more predictable.

Structuring, ...

If a company is fully funded by equity, there is no structuring. All the risk from the asset side carries over one-to-one to the shareholders. But as soon as a company finances its assets with any form of credit, *structuring* happens. In this case, the liability side of the company consists of debt and equity.

The risk that is inherent to the assets is unevenly distributed between lenders and shareholders. Shareholders suffer losses first;

they carry more risk than debt holders. Lenders only start losing money if the equity is completely eradicated.

Structuring redistributes credit risk from lenders to shareholders. As we will see later, the liability side can be further structured by issuing junior and senior forms of debt. Similar to shareholders, junior debt holders serve as a buffer before senior debt holders have to suffer losses. Senior debt holders are protected from some losses by junior debt holders and shareholders.[13]

Collateralization, and ...

Recall that a lender can ask the borrower to put up collateral. If the borrower is not able to fully repay the loan, the collateral can be claimed, sold, and used to cover the losses from the loan. Since the asset used as collateral is initially owned by the borrower, he runs the risk of losing in the event of default on the loan. Collateralization moves risk from the lender back to the borrower.

Insurance

Financial institutions can obtain financial insurance from third parties for the liabilities or the equity they issued. The third party promises to make up for potential losses on the insured claims. *Insurance* moves credit risk from the insured claim holders to the insuring third party.

Government guarantees—in the form of lender-of-last-resort policy or deposit insurance—are a form of insurance. They are the ultimate financial insurance. In a fiat monetary regime, the central bank can issue as much outside money as required to uphold banking guarantees. Holders of claims insured by the government can anticipate receiving the full nominal amount promised.[14]

Diversification, structuring, collateralization, and insurance can create very safe liabilities and equity shares. Nevertheless, they cannot completely eradicate risk. In an uncertain world, risk diversification is sometimes ineffective due to unexpected correlation. Structuring might be insufficient to protect senior credit from losses, collateral can lose value, or insuring institutions can fail. Residual risk always remains. In times of financial tranquility, however, financial institutions can create credit that is generally perceived as risk-free.[15]

The Transformation of Maturity by Offering Contractual Liquidity

Transforming the size of credit and removing most of its credit risk does not suffice to create inside money. To become inside money, credit has to become as liquid as money. Inside money has to be convertible into outside money at par and at any time. For this, the financial technique of maturity transformation needs to be applied to an extent that credit features contractual liquidity. By *contractual liquidity*, we mean the promise of financial institutions to redeem credit instantly at par upon notice from the lender.[16]

Contractual liquidity is conceptually different from market liquidity. By *market liquidity*, we mean the liquidity of an asset traded on a market. Why is this so? Market-traded assets are sold at a market price that fluctuates depending on supply and demand. Market liquidity emerges from the interaction between market participants who are free to buy and sell assets at any price they deem appropriate. In contrast, credit featuring contractual liquidity can be "sold" back to the borrower any time and at a fixed price. Contractual liquidity emerges from a contractual obligation.[17]

By applying the six financial techniques of banking—pooling, diversification, structuring, collateralization, insurance, and contractual liquidity—every company with a balance sheet can create money out of credit. The techniques do not need to be performed on one single balance sheet. Information technology allows banking over a series of interlinked balance sheets. This is what shadow banking is all about.

--------------------------------- NOTES ---------------------------------

1. For an overview article on the effects of information technology on finance, see Allen, McAndrews, and Strahan (2002).

2. Our definition is close to Pozsar et al. (2013, 1) who write that "shadow banking activities consist of credit, maturity, and liquidity transformation that take place without direct and explicit access to public sources of liquidity or credit backstops."

3. See Cook and Duffield (1979).

4. See D. Jones (2000).

5. Jackson et al. (1999, 26). We explain securitization in greater detail in the next chapter.

6. Jackson et al. (1999, 2).

7. The term *boundary problem* was coined by Goodhart (2008).

8. For instance, many trust companies have been established in the years before the financial crisis of 1907—the crisis that catalyzed the creation of the Federal Reserve System. These companies conducted banking, but were not banks in a legal sense (Carlson 2013).

9. See Kane (1981, 360) who compiled a list of selected substitutes for regulated banking activities that was already impressive in the 1980s.

10. Our concept of inside money loosely follows the concept of information insensitivity, first developed by Gorton and Pennacchi (1990). They emphasize that some forms of safe securitized debt can "be used by uninformed agents for transaction purposes" (p. 51). In a later account, Gorton, Lewellen, and Metrick (2012, 9) use the term *money-like debt* to refer to "commercial paper, net repurchase agreements, federal funds, money market mutual fund assets, interbank transactions, broker-dealer payables, and broker-dealer security credits."

11. This point is not entirely true for collateralization, given that it not only transforms risk but also changes the incentives for the borrower who puts his or her collateral at risk (see our discussion of excessive risk taking in Chapter 3). Collateralization can thus be considered as a hybrid of risk reduction and transformation. Further, note that structuring and insurance may, *over time,* raise aggregate credit risk in the economy due to moral hazard behavior, that is, excessive risk taking.

12. Let us give an example here. One household that exactly grants one loan to one firm runs the risk of losing everything if this firm goes bankrupt. If 100 such households pool their savings, they could then grant loans to 100 firms. If one firm still goes bankrupt, the losses are shared among all households. The individual risk of each loan must not be perfectly correlated for diversification to make sense.

13. Shareholders and junior debt holders carry more risks than senior ones. This risk is compensated by higher returns. The mechanisms at work in this shifting of risk and return can be explored in Modigliani and Miller (1958).

14. Even the government, however, cannot insure the *real* value of credit contracts, a point we come back to later.

15. The term *financial tranquility* is from Minsky (1986).

16. Liquidity, in general, is the ease with which an asset can be exchanged with other goods, services, or assets. Since outside money is accepted for virtually all economic transactions, it can be regarded as the most liquid asset of all. Hence, we can redefine liquidity in terms of outside money and consider an asset to be liquid if one can exchange it with little or no costs into outside money.

17. Credit with contractual liquidity has an additional characteristic: It does not feature any interest rate risk. The value of credit with immediate maturity is insensitive to interest rate changes. To see this, assume that you lent money when interest rates were low with a maturity date of two years. Now imagine that interest rates increase just after you granted the loan. If you still had the money, you could now lend the money at a higher rate. But you cannot get your money back before maturity. If you had added a clause in the loan contract that the borrower has to repay you the loan immediately at notice, you would not have to face this problem. You would call up the borrower, demand your money, and lend it at the now higher interest rate to someone else, or even to the same borrower.

5 The Mechanics of Shadow Banking

At the turn of the millennium, shadow banking in the United States created inside money in a series of steps over a number of balance sheets. A comprehensive explanation of shadow banking is beyond the scope of this book. This is why we focus on two channels of shadow banking that played a prominent role in the financial crisis of 2007–08.[1]

Even our short introduction is rather technical, though. Both the basic technicalities and some notation is indispensable to understand the financial crisis of 2007–08. We provide a stylized example at the end of the chapter that helps to grasp the mechanics of shadow banking.

At the beginning of shadow banking stands loan origination. To create inside money, one needs to extend credit first. Shadow and traditional banking are not different at this point. Loans that end up in the shadow banking sector as "raw material" have either been granted by a traditional bank or by another financial institution. A single loan is usually rather risky, and securitization, addresses this issue.

Securitization

Securitization combines three financial techniques of banking: pooling, diversification, and structuring. In the first step, banks or other financial institutions establish—in financial terms, *sponsor*—a limited liability company. In the context of securitization, this limited liability company is called a *special purpose vehicle* (SPV). An SPV is a legal entity that neither produces anything nor offers any services nor employs any people. It is only a remote balance sheet that buys a diversified portfolio of illiquid loans from the sponsoring institution. The asset side of the SPV's balance sheet does not differ much from the asset side of a bank's balance sheet.

The liability side, however, is different from the one of a bank. The SPV does not issue bank deposits. If it did, it would just be a bank and, consequently, subject to banking regulations. Rather, the SPV issues debt in the form of *asset-backed securities* (ABSs). They are backed by a diversified portfolio of loans on the asset side, hence the name.

The financial institution that originated the loans has now successfully transformed the notional amount of its illiquid loans; it pooled them on the asset side of an SPV and issued ABSs with a standardized notional amount. Let us assume that this financial institution wants to sell the ABSs to raise money.[2] Not knowing much about the quality of the underlying loans, a potential buyer might be reluctant to buy. An asymmetric information problem exists between the sponsoring institution selling ABSs and the potential buyer.

The sponsoring institution tackles this issue with another financial technique. It structures the liability side of the SPV. The sponsoring institution typically holds an equity tranche and thus suffers the first losses if the loan quality is poor. The liability side of the SPV can be structured even further by issuing ABSs with different seniority. In financial terms, this is called *tranching*. The tranche with the highest seniority is serviced first, then the second highest, and so on.[3] Finally, the different ABS tranches are rated by an external rating agency to provide an independent confirmation that the credit-risk transformation has been successful.

Although securitization removes the loans from the balance sheet of the sponsoring institution, much of the credit-risk exposure of the loans of an ABS remains with the very same institution. The sponsoring institution usually holds the equity and junior tranches and, hence, suffers losses first. As such, the main motivation for banks to securitize is not to remove risk from their balance sheet, but regulatory capital arbitrage. This is the boundary problem at work. Circumventing capital requirements has been a major incentive for traditional banks to securitize their loans.[4]

Securitization is the process of pooling together various assets into SPVs and issuing securities with different credit risk. Above, we have explained this process with loans on the asset side of the SPV. But creative financial institutions do not stop at this point. The whole process also works with ABSs as assets in the first place. Financial institutions have sponsored SPVs that pool multiple ABSs on the asset side. The SPVs then issue yet another three-letter security called a *collateralized debt obligation* (CDO) on the liability side. While ABSs are backed by loans, CDOs are backed by ABSs.

Usually, higher risk ABS tranches that would have otherwise remained on the balance sheet of the sponsoring institutions are pooled into CDOs. Doing so, banks can further optimize capital requirements. Securitization can be applied again on CDOs. High-risk CDOs can be pooled in yet another SPV. After another round of securitization, the new product is called CDO squared (CDO^2). If you repeat the process one more time, you end up with CDO cubed (CDO^3). Figure 5.1 illustrates the securitization chain from loans to CDO^2.

We will not go into more detail here.[5] The key takeaway is that loans can be securitized. Be it ABS, CDO, CDO^2, or CDO^3, it always starts with loans to households and businesses. Securitization—pooling, diversification, and structuring on SPVs' balance sheets—then transforms these loans into (seemingly) safe assets while concentrating credit risk in equity and junior tranches that are held by the sponsoring institutions, which are often banks.

Securitization usually does not transform maturities. That is, ABSs and CDOs are of long-term maturity as are the underlying loans. Securitization is only the first step to create money out of credit; the next step is the transformation of maturity.

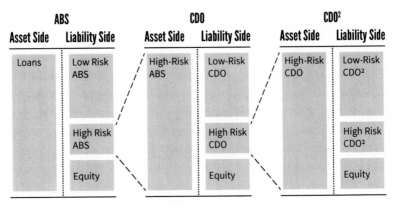

Figure 5.1 The securitization chain

Repurchase Agreements

We encountered repurchase agreements (repos) when we discussed central banks. Repos are used not only as a tool of monetary policy by central banks but also as a tool for short-term borrowing and lending by financial institutions. A repo is similar to a collateralized loan. Nevertheless, there is an important legal difference between the two: A repo is a sale of an asset combined with a later purchase of the same asset. This seemingly small difference stems from bankruptcy regulation. If a borrower defaults, the repo lender legally owns the collateral immediately without having to claim it in bankruptcy procedures. The repo lender can sell the collateral instantly on the market to recover the loss on the repo loan. In contrast, the lender of a collateralized loan has to participate in the bankruptcy procedures of the borrower. The absence of legal uncertainties makes repo lending attractive.

A repo is usually collateralized with financial assets that feature high market liquidity.[6] If the borrower defaults, the repo lender can sell the collateral quickly and does not have to worry about current market conditions. Therefore, the repo lender will request a security as collateral that is considered very safe, such as a U.S. Treasury bond or a highly rated ABS or CDO.

Even relatively safe and liquid securities, however, can lose value if market conditions deteriorate. In this case, the collateral no longer fully protects a repo lender from credit risk. Overcollateralization addresses this problem. Repo lenders request collateral with a market value that exceeds the notional amount of the loan. The difference is called a "haircut" and is expressed in percentage points. With a 10% haircut and collateral with a market price of $100, the actual repo amounts to $90.

If we put repos back into the perspective of shadow banking, we see that they take over two functions. First, by applying a haircut to the ABS or CDO used as collateral, repos transform credit risk. Lending via repo against an ABS as collateral is safer than holding the ABS itself. Credit risk is almost eliminated during times of financial tranquility.

Second, repos transform maturity. Many repos have an overnight maturity and are rolled over—that is, automatically extended another day—if wished by the lender. Such an arrangement is a form of contractual liquidity. When repo lenders decide to withdraw their money, they just stop rolling over the repos. Repo lending is very safe and features contractual liquidity; a repo feels almost as good as money for the repo lender.[7]

Let us recap. Illiquid loans are securitized into ABSs and CDOs, which can then be used as collateral in repos. Squinting a bit and looking at the big picture, we realize that risky long-term loans are funded with virtually risk-free credit featuring contractual liquidity. It seems like we are already quite close to creating money out of credit.

Money Market Mutual Funds

Large nonfinancial companies, pension funds, and wealthy individuals do not rely exclusively on bank deposits. Further, they rarely engage in repos. Rather, such investors buy MMMF shares. MMMFs advertise their shares as being risk-free and redeemable at par any time; that is, they offer contractual liquidity. MMMF shares constitute inside money. They are the deposit contracts of shadow banking, which is underscored by the fact that many MMMF fund providers offer payment services.[8]

MMMFs are major repo lenders.[9] If some investors want to re-deem their MMMF shares, the MMMF manager simply does not roll over a few repos. With the proceeds, the manager can honor the promise of contractual liquidity.

Contrary to a traditional bank, an MMMF does not directly grant loans, because that would undermine its promise of instant maturity and absence of risk, and it might also bring bank regula-tors to the scene. Indirectly, however, MMMF shares finance loans via two channels, one of which we have just discussed. In Figure 5.2, we have visualized the first channel of shadow banking.

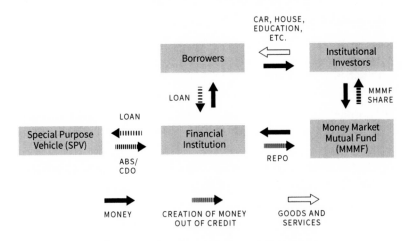

Figure 5.2 *Shadow banking: the repo channel*

Let us now turn to the second channel. MMMFs invest in other assets in addition to repos. Repos are safe and feature short matur-ities, but they offer only low returns. If MMMFs invested in repos only, they would struggle to attract sufficient demand from inves-tors. Similar to banks not expecting all their depositors to withdraw their money at the same time, MMMFs do not expect all their shares to be redeemed at once. Hence, MMMFs invest a material fraction of their funds in slightly riskier and longer dated assets such as *as-set-backed commercial paper (ABCP)*.[10]

Asset-Backed Commercial Paper

ABCP conduits pool ABSs on the asset side and issue ABCPs on the liability side of their balance sheet.[11] ABCPs are usually rated by rating agencies. ABCP conduits are SPVs, and at first sight, an ABCP conduit could be mistaken for an SPV that issues CDOs.

However, ABCPs and CDOs have some fundamental differences. First, ABCPs are of very large denominations.[12] Second, many ABCPs are backed by explicit or implicit credit guarantees; that is, ABCP conduits are insured by the sponsoring institutions against losses.[13] Third, ABCP conduits transform maturities. In the end, ABCP conduits resemble traditional banks that offer deposits with large notional amounts.

Transforming maturities comes at the price of liquidity risk. Most ABCPs have a maturity of a few days. Hence, ABCP conduits have to continuously roll over ABCPs to finance the underlying as-

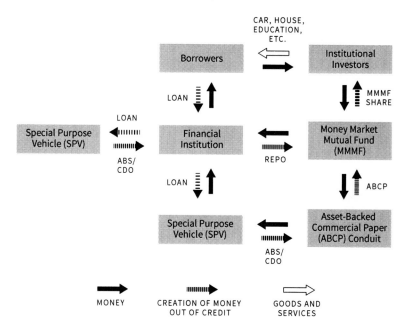

Figure 5.3 Shadow banking: the repo and the ABCP channel

sets. To mitigate liquidity risk, the sponsoring institution provides liquidity guarantees in addition to credit guarantees. If the conduit is unable to find new buyers for its ABCPs, the sponsor steps in. As long as both credit and liquidity guarantees are credible, MMMFs perceive ABCPs as risk-free and, hence, as a suitable and attractive investment. Figure 5.3 includes the second channel of shadow banking.

While ABCP conduits remove ABSs from a bank balance sheet, the sponsoring institutions still carry the main portion of the credit and liquidity risks involved. But ABCP conduits have been legally set up in a way that the banks sponsoring them can optimize their regulatory capital. Capital requirements for providing liquidity and credit guarantees to ABCP conduits are lower than those for actually holding the respective ABSs. Again and again, we see the boundary problem of financial regulation at work.[14]

A Stylized Example of Shadow Banking

Compared to traditional banking, shadow banking is obscure and complex. We had to introduce an alphabet soup of abbreviations to explain the two major shadow banking channels. It is difficult to grasp all the details immediately. In what follows, we present a simple and stylized example of shadow banking. We hope this helps to cut through the complexity.

Recall the example we used to explain traditional banking in Part One. Let us consider the same setup within a shadow banking setting with securitization, repos, and MMMFs. Again, Alex opens a bank by providing $80 of outside money as equity, and Sarah successfully applies for a loan of $60.

In the digital age, Sarah no longer keeps her money in a bank deposit. Instead, she has an MMMF account. She buys 60 shares with a denomination of $1 from the MMMF operated by Michelle. Michelle promises Sarah she will buy back shares any time for $1. For Sarah, the MMMF shares feel as good as money.

Again, Sarah buys a coffee roaster from Ryan. Ryan also has an account with Michelle's MMMF. Sarah and Ryan consider it cum-

1. Sarah obtains a loan and deposits the money into her MMMF account.

Asset Side	MMMF	Liability Side		Asset Side	Bank	Liability Side
60	Cash	Shares Sarah 60		20	Cash	
				60	Loan to Sarah	
						Equity Alex 80
60	Total	Total 60		80	Total	Total 80

2. Sarah buys a coffee roaster from Ryan, using the MMMF's payment services.

Asset Side	MMMF	Liability Side		Asset Side	Bank	Liability Side
60	Cash	Shares Sarah 0		20	Cash	
		Shares Ryan 60		60	Loan to Sarah	
						Equity Alex 80
60	Total	Total 60		80	Total	Total 80

3. Alex securitizes Sarah's loan.

Asset Side	MMMF	Liability Side		Asset Side	Bank	Liability Side
60	Cash	Shares Sarah 0		20	Cash	
		Shares Ryan 60		54	ABS Sarah	
				6	Equity SPV	Equity Alex 80
60	Total	Total 60		80	Total	Total 80

4. Alex borrows money from the MMMF with a repo.

Asset Side	MMMF	Liability Side		Asset Side	Bank	Liability Side
11	Cash	Shares Sarah 0		69	Cash	Repo 49
49	Repo	Shares Ryan 60		54	ABS Sarah	
				6	Equity SPV	Equity Alex 80
60	Total	Total 60		129	Total	Total 129

Figure 5.4 Money creation by shadow banking: part one

bersome to sell shares, exchange physical cash, and then buy shares again. Instead, they simply advise Michelle to transfer the ownership of 60 shares from Sarah to Ryan.

In the meantime, Julia notifies Alex that she would like to borrow $60 to get her coffee roasting business going. While Alex would like to grant the loan, he does not have enough cash to do so. Hence, he securitizes Sarah's loan: He sponsors an SPV and transfers the loan of Sarah to the asset side of the SPV. Alex then structures the liability side of the SPV into $6 of equity and an ABS worth $54. Both the equity tranche and the ABS are moved back on the balance sheet of his bank.

Alex structured the SPV to transform the credit risk of Sarah's loan. Protected by the equity buffer, the ABS features lower credit risk than Sarah's loan. Alex then has the credit risk certified by a credit-rating agency. With a good rating indicating the low credit risk, the ABS can be used by Alex as collateral in a repo to raise cash.

Alex calls Michelle to propose a repo transaction. Michelle is happy to do so, as she has $60 sitting idle on the asset side of her MMMF's balance sheet. They agree on the ABS as collateral and on an overnight maturity. For Michelle, the repo allows her to invest her cash, while she is still able to honor the promise she made to her shareholders. If they want to redeem their shares, she just stops rolling over the repo.

Still, Michelle is a bit concerned. In case Alex defaults, the ABS might lose value, and she might not recoup the losses. She addresses her concern by charging a 10% haircut; that is, she only lends $49 to Alex using an ABS with a value of $54 as collateral. Figure 5.4 illustrates what is happening on the balance sheets of Alex's bank and of Michelle's MMMF.

In the economy of our example, we now have $60 of inside money in the form of MMMF shares. As demonstrated, MMMF shares can be used to make payments. Furthermore, Alex's bank has $69 at its disposal. Alex can now grant the loan to Julia. She successfully applies for a loan of $60 and also buys shares from Michelle's MMMF. Then she calls up Ryan and buys a coffee roaster by transferring her MMMF shares.

5. Julia obtains a loan and deposits it in the MMMF as well.

Asset Side	MMMF	Liability Side		Asset Side	Bank	Liability Side	
71	Cash	Shares Sarah	0	9	Cash	Repo	49
49	Repo	Shares Julia	60	54	ABS Sarah		
		Shares Ryan	60	60	Loan Julia		
				6	Equity SPV	Equity Alex	80
120	Total	Total	120	129	Total	Total	129

6. Julia buys a coffee roaster from Ryan, using the MMMF's payment services.

Asset Side	MMMF	Liability Side		Asset Side	Bank	Liability Side	
71	Cash	Shares Sarah	0	9	Cash	Repo	49
49	Repo	Shares Ryan	120	54	ABS Sarah		
		Shares Julia	0	60	Loan Julia		
				6	Equity SPV	Equity Alex	80
120	Total	Total	120	129	Total	Total	129

7. Alex securitizes Julia's loan.

Asset Side	MMMF	Liability Side		Asset Side	Bank	Liability Side	
71	Cash	Shares Sarah	0	9	Cash	Repo	49
49	Repo	Shares Ryan	120	54	ABS Sarah		
		Shares Julia	0	54	ABS Julia		
				12	Equity SPV	Equity Alex	80
120	Total	Total	120	129	Total	Total	129

8. Alex borrows more money from the MMMF via repo.

Asset Side	MMMF	Liability Side		Asset Side	Bank	Liability Side	
22	Cash	Shares Sarah	0	58	Cash	Repo	98
98	Repo	Shares Ryan	120	54	ABS Sarah		
		Shares Julia	0	54	ABS Julia		
				12	Equity SPV	Equity Alex	80
120	Total	Total	120	178	Total	Total	178

Figure 5.5 *Money creation by shadow banking: part two*

Alex would like to grant even more loans. He securitizes Julia's loan again, just as he did with Sarah's loan. He transfers Julia's loan into an SPV, and creates an ABS backed by Julia's loan and protected by an equity buffer. He obtains a credit rating and uses the ABS to borrow more money via repo from Michelle with the same conditions as before. Figure 5.5 visualizes the events.

We can see that the amount of inside money has increased. After two rounds, $120 of inside money was created by shadow banking in the form of MMMF shares. Assume that Valerie is another coffee-roasting entrepreneur who would like to obtain a loan of $60. After the second round of securitization, Alex can no longer grant such a loan. Inside money creation in the shadow banking sector cannot continue endlessly.

Contrary to today's money creation by banks, no legal constraints such as reserve or capital requirements restrict inside money creation. Credit risk perceptions by market participants determine how large both the equity share in securitization and the haircut in repo transactions have to be. This constrains how much money can be created by shadow banking. With lower equity buffers and haircuts, shadow banking can create more inside money.

As in traditional banking, the process of money creation can reverse itself. Let us assume that Ryan buys freshly roasted coffee from Sarah for $60. He does so by transferring 60 shares of Michelle's MMMF back to Sarah. At the same time, Sarah's loan becomes due, and she asks Michelle to redeem her shares. Michelle stops rolling over one of the two repos she has outstanding with Alex and raises $49 of cash. Together with her previous cash reserve, she can buy back 60 shares from Sarah at the promised price of $1. As Michelle stopped rolling the repo, Alex has now the respective ABS back in his custody. As the loan becomes due, he reverses the securitization. Sarah pays back her loan, and the amount of inside money decreases. Figure 5.6 illustrates the steps of money destruction.

Our example highlights two features of shadow banking that are inherent in all forms of banking. First, a money multiplier is at work that depends on the credit-risk perception of financial market

9. Ryan buys freshly roasted coffee from Sarah.

Asset Side	MMMF	Liability Side		Asset Side	Bank		Liability Side
22	Cash	Shares Sarah	60	58	Cash	Repo	98
98	Repo	Shares Ryan	60	54	ABS Sarah		
		Shares Julia	0	54	ABS Julia		
				12	Equity SPV	Equity Alex	80
120	Total	Total	120	178	Total	Total	178

10. The repo on Sarah's ABS is not rolled over.

Asset Side	MMMF	Liability Side		Asset Side	Bank		Liability Side
71	Cash	Shares Sarah	60	9	Cash	Repo	49
49	Repo	Shares Ryan	60	54	ABS Sarah		
		Shares Julia	0	54	ABS Julia		
				12	Equity SPV	Equity Alex	80
120	Total	Total	120	129	Total	Total	129

11. Alex reverses the securitization and puts Sarah's loan back on his balance sheet.

Asset Side	MMMF	Liability Side		Asset Side	Bank		Liability Side
71	Cash	Shares Sarah	60	9	Cash	Repo	49
49	Repo	Shares Ryan	60	60	Loan Sarah		
		Shares Julia	0	54	ABS Julia		
				6	Equity SPV	Equity Alex	80
120	Total	Total	120	129	Total	Total	129

12. Sarah withdraws her MMMF share and pays back her loan.

Asset Side	MMMF	Liability Side		Asset Side	Bank		Liability Side
11	Cash	Shares Sarah	0	69	Cash	Repo	49
49	Repo	Shares Ryan	60	0	Loan Sarah		
		Shares Julia	0	54	ABS Julia		
				6	Equity SPV	Equity Alex	80
60	Total	Total	60	129	Total	Total	129

Figure 5.6 Money destruction by shadow banking

participants. In the case of the first shadow banking channel, the risk perceptions materialize in the size of the equity buffer necessary for securitization and on the haircut applied by the repo lenders. During the boom years before the financial crisis of 2007–08, haircuts for ABS sometimes dropped to 0%, and riskier ABS tranches were resecuritized in CDOs that could be used for repo transactions, too. Such low levels of credit protection allow for a rapid expansion of credit and inside money. In our example, Alex would not have been cash constrained after having granted loans to Sarah and Julia. Valerie could have obtained a loan from Alex's bank, and further inside money would have been created.

Second, the virtuous circle of money creation can turn vicious. Shadow banking features the same weaknesses as traditional banking. If too many MMMF shareholders and repo lenders "withdraw" their money at once, a shadow banking panic can happen. In the end, the fundamental weakness of banking is always the same. All banking is prone to bank runs and banking panics. Without government guarantees, it was only a matter of time until a shadow banking panic would happen: the financial crisis of 2007–08.

NOTES

1. For more details on shadow banking, see Pozsar et al. (2013).

2. This business model is called *originate to distribute*. In contrast, the traditional banking business of keeping loans on the balance sheet is described as *take and hold*.

3. In the context of shadow banking, these techniques are commonly described as *credit enhancement*.

4. See Jackson et al. (1999) and D. Jones (2000).

5. See Gorton and Souleles (2007) and Coval, Jurek, and Stafford (2009) for further information. For an accessible account on how subprime mortgage CDO markets worked until the crisis, see Lewis (2011).

6. Bankruptcy laws specify the securities that repo lenders are allowed to claim without going through the normal bankruptcy process. Since the 1980s, the U.S. Congress has allowed more and more securities to be used as collateral in repos. In 2005, Congress

enacted the Bankruptcy Abuse Prevention and Consumer Protection Act, which allows the use of mortgage-related securities in repos. See Acharya and Öncü (2010) for a comprehensive overview of repo market regulation.

7. See Gorton (2010) or Gorton and Metrick (2012) for an extensive discussion of repos and their role in the financial crisis of 2007–08.

8. MMMFs are not the only way to tap the money market. There are, for example, also enhanced cash funds; see Pozsar et al. (2010). For ease of exposition, we focus exclusively on MMMFs. MMMFs are regulated by the U.S. Securities and Exchange Commission (SEC) and are only allowed to invest in short-term and high-rated debt. MMMFs are the only mutual funds that are excluded from the obligation to mark their assets daily according to current market prices (mark-to-market). They can mark their assets at par with the so-called amortized-cost accounting method (Birdthistle 2010, 1174–75). Investors refer to MMMFs as $1 net asset value funds, because their core promise is to always pay out the deposited dollar fully at any time. If unable to live up to this promise, an MMMF is said to "break the buck."

9. See Macey (2011).

10. See Covitz, Liang, and Suarez (2013).

11. There are also ABCPs that are backed by loans. These vehicles did not play a material role in the financial crisis of 2007–08; see Arteta et al. (2013).

12. In contrast to CDOs, ABCPs are not securities. ABCPs are a sophisticated form of *commercial papers* (CPs). CPs are explicitly not securities and cannot be sold in small denominations to retail investors. As such, they are exempted from costly regulation by the SEC. This is why CPs are popular among public companies to raise short term-funding from large investors. See also Anderson and Gascon (2009, 590).

13. See Arteta et al. (2013). For example, sponsors promised to support the ABCP conduit in case it suffers any losses. As we will see in the next chapter, numerous banks suffered massive losses due to these credit guarantees for ABCP conduits.

14. See Acharya, Schnabl, and Suarez (2013).

<u>6</u> The Financial Crisis of 2007–08

The mechanics of shadow banking are opaque and hard to grasp. It is no wonder that regulators did not realize the threat of a banking panic originating in the shadow banking sector. The regulators' negligence partly explains why the regulatory framework in place at the eve of the financial crisis of 2007–08 was not suited to prevent a shadow banking panic.

The Regulatory Framework

Regulators did not see any need for shadow banking regulation before the crisis. They argued that without explicit banking guarantees in place, the threat of failure would impose sufficient "market discipline" on financial institutions that operated outside the regulated banking sector. As securitization and ABCP conduits seemingly transferred credit risk away from banks, financial innovation was perceived as a stabilizing factor to the financial system and the economy.[1]

Nevertheless, even the most optimistic regulators acknowledged that capital requirements à la Basel I lost much of their effectiveness.[2] Banks moved assets off their balance sheets, but kept large portions of the risk. Regulators tried to update capital requirements so that they would account for the way traditional banks operate in the digital age. These efforts resulted in the second Basel Capital Accord, called Basel II.[3]

The guiding principle of Basel II was that a bank's capital requirement should depend on the "true" market, credit, and operational risks. The Basel Committee on Banking Supervision introduced several changes in the risk-weighting methodology to achieve this. First, they encouraged banks to set up sophisticated internal risk systems. Second, capital requirements were refined to better accommodate securitization and the insurances provided to the shadow banking sector. Finally, more power was given to external credit-rating agencies.

The original text of Basel II contains more than 300 pages. Various updates, amendments, and national guidelines followed—thousands of pages in all. The complexity of banking regulation exploded. Implementing and supervising the highly sophisticated rules required tremendous efforts by highly skilled employees on both the banks' and the regulators' sides.[4]

Note that while Basel II became effective only shortly before the financial crisis of 2007–08, banks had started implementing it earlier. Many of the suggested measures of Basel II had already been in place at the beginning of the crisis, but the devastating run of events could not be prevented. Moreover, Basel II had some unintended consequences that affected the way the crisis unfolded.

Still Not Enough Skin in the Game

As we have mentioned, Basel II encouraged banks to develop sophisticated risk-management systems. Allowing banks to use their own risk management to determine their capital requirements, however, turned out to be almost the same as letting banks decide for themselves how much capital to hold. Banking regulation cannot build on the collaboration of banks that enjoy government guarantees, as they would like to take as much risk as possible. The then chairman of the Federal Deposit Insurance Corporation (FDIC) described it as follows: "That would be like a football match where each player has his own set of rules. There are strong reasons for believing that banks left to their own devices would maintain less capital—not more—than would be prudent."[5]

It is not surprising that Basel II reduced the effective capital requirements for banks compared to Basel I. In 2006, the Bank of International Settlement published a quantitative impact study (QIS). It became clear that Basel II led to decreases in actual capital requirements: "The QIS results for the G10 countries show that minimum required capital under Basel II … would decrease relative to the current Accord."[6] A study of the FDIC expected "large percentage reductions in risk-based capital requirements" if Basel II was fully implemented for U.S. banks.[7] Basel II blatantly failed to achieve its main goal; banks managed to hold even less equity than under Basel I. Unfortunately, outsourcing some of the risk management to rating agencies did not help either

Flawed Rating of Shadow Banking Products

In the industrial age, rating agencies provided independent credit risk assessments of countries and companies. Such a risk assessment is costly, and somebody has to pay for it. Until the 1970s, rating agencies applied an *investor pays* model. Technological progress — among other things — forced rating agencies to change their business model and switch to an *issuer pays* model.[8]

A conflict of interest arises with such a model. The one paying for the rating service is interested in an optimistic rather than an accurate rating. This conflict of interest is mitigated by a reputation effect. Reputation is a valuable asset for a rating agency. If it consistently provides too optimistic ratings, it loses investors' trust. Its ratings are no longer perceived as useful, and issuers of securities stop paying for them.

Depending on the trade-off between the short-term profits of pleasing an issuer and the long-term costs of reputation damage, it is often the better choice for a rating agency to stick to a correct rating and protect its reputation. Rating agencies have applied the issuer pays model for quite some time, and it worked well for company and country ratings.[9]

However, ratings of shadow banking products — such as ABSs and CDOs — have turned out to be seriously flawed. The ratings of countries and companies are easier to understand than the ratings of shadow banking products. If a rating agency attaches a high credit rating to an indebted company with an unsound business model, competitors and other informed investors will quickly find out that the rating is flawed.

The complexity of shadow banking products has made it difficult for investors to independently assess the quality of the credit rating. As we have just seen, the underlying mechanics are hard to grasp. Only a few insiders knew what was actually bundled into shadow banking products. It was hard for outsiders to judge the quality of ratings, and it took people a long time to find out that some of them were seriously inflated.[10]

When it came to rate shadow banking products, the trade-off between short-term profits and long-term reputation leaned toward short-term profits. Rating agencies were willing to put their reputation at risk to increase their revenues with generous ratings in the profitable market for shadow banking products.[11] Moral hazard made its way into the rating agencies business.

The U.S. Securities and Exchange Commission (SEC) investigated the role of rating agencies in the financial crisis of 2007–08. The SEC revealed that rating agencies rated complex shadow banking products despite knowing that this practice strained both their personnel and their intellectual capacity. Furthermore, rating agencies were well aware that their rating models did not incorporate all relevant parameters.[12]

Moral hazard in rating shadow banking products resulted in inflated ratings across the board. Issuers knew of rating agencies' weaknesses, and they systematically exploited these when designing shadow banking products. They managed to obtain the highest possible rating despite high risks.[13] Rating agencies failed to assess the true economic risks of shadow banking products.[14]

Rating agencies emphasize that their ratings are mere opinions.[15] With the implementation of Basel II, however, their opinions became official determinants of banks' regulatory capital requirements. If the rating for an asset is high, less capital needs to be put up for holding it, and vice versa.

When the financial crisis of 2007–08 hit, the value of shadow banking products fell much faster than was to be expected by their rating. Equity put up by banks for buffering such losses was insufficient. This brought many banks to the brink of bankruptcy and thus threatened to bring down the whole financial system.

Similar to encouraging sophisticated risk-management systems for determining capital requirements, integrating rating agencies into banking regulation turned out to be a bad idea. To make things worse, Basel II had even more unintended consequences. Probably the most problematic one was that Basel II fostered the rise of huge global banks.

Large Banks Benefited from New Rules

The size of large banks has increased dramatically over recent years, and the banking sector has become more concentrated than ever. The number of U.S. banks was almost cut in half from more than 12,000 in 1990 to around 7,000 in 2009. In the United States, the share of the four largest banks in total bank assets increased from about 14% to over 40% from 1992 to 2009.[16] Today, a few players dominate the global financial system. Two regulatory measures encouraged this development: deposit insurance and Basel II.

The effect of deposit insurance on the market concentration of banks is an indirect one. In business, and actually in everybody's life, some projects succeed and some do not. Consequently, some banks fail for a variety of reasons. If they were nonbank companies, they would file for bankruptcy, and life would go on. For banks with insured deposits, however, things look different.

To minimize the costs of dealing with bank failure, the FDIC sometimes merges failing banks with financially healthy banks. This seems to be a good idea, since unwinding all the positions of a bank is costly and implies legal litigation that can go on for years. Organizing a merge with a stable bank alleviates these costs.[17] However, if you repeatedly merge failing banks with healthy ones, you inevitably end up with fewer and larger banks.

While deposit insurance led to mergers and, in turn, larger banks, Basel II created a competitive advantage for large banks. Only large banks can afford to set up internal risk-management systems. Hundreds of qualified people such as lawyers, accountants, and quantitative-risk managers are required to calculate capital requirements based on the internal rating approach. Basel II still allowed banks to use a standardized approach that did not require internal risk-management systems. The standardized approach, however, resulted in higher capital requirements.[18] As such, Basel II puts tighter restrictions on small banks than on large ones.

In addition, Basel II incentivizes large banks to grow even further because internal risk-management systems create high fixed costs. No matter how many assets a bank holds, it always has to cover these costs. If a bank sets up a risk-management system that effectively saves regulatory capital, every further asset acquired benefits from it. Put simply, once you have managed to exploit some regulatory loopholes, you can use this trick for every additional dollar on your balance sheet.

Amplification of Business Cycles

One more item has to be added to the list of Basel II's unintended consequences. Basel II approached banking from a microeconomic perspective. Regulators focused on the single bank. The underlying idea was that if individual banks were in sound condition, the banking system as a whole would be in sound condition. Such a microeconomic approach, however, turned out to amplify business cycles and undermine the stability of the financial system in its entirety.[19]

Internal risk-management models that have been promoted by Basel II use statistical models to determine the capital requirement. Various input parameters are required to calculate the risk weight for a given asset. The four basic input parameters are the probability of default, the loss given default, the exposure at default, and the effective maturity. The higher these parameters are, the higher is credit risk, and, correspondingly, the higher are capital requirements.[20]

Internal risk-management models typically neither assess default probabilities nor loss given default of borrowers over the whole business cycle, but rather at a particular point in time. During booms, such a model reports low default probabilities, while in a crisis, default probabilities increase. As a result, capital requirements are low in good times and high in bad times.[21]

At the peak of a boom, shortly before the economy slips into a recession and the capital buffer to absorb losses should be high, the effective capital requirements become lowest. Banks can extend credit on generous terms and expand their balance sheets further. Increased availability of credit and inside money amplifies the boom.

When a crisis hits, however, input parameters start indicating higher credit risk, and effective capital requirements become tighter. Banks deleverage in order to cope with tighter capital requirements. The banking system reduces the supply of credit and inside money. The recession worsens, and input parameters indicate even more credit risk. The previous virtuous circle turns into a vicious one.

A Chronology of the Events

In accordance with the saying "out of sight, out of mind," some experts were calling the steady economic development since the mid-1980s the *great moderation*. But shadow banking is just as exposed to banking panics as traditional banking. What happened to traditional banking in 1907 and in the 1930s had to happen eventually to shadow banking. But first things first, the story of the financial crisis of 2007–08 started with an unsustainable boom caused by unregulated shadow banking.

The Shadow Banking Boom ...

Recall how shadow banking transforms risky long-term credit into inside money. Loans are originated and then securitized into shadow banking products such as ABSs and CDOs. The shadow banking products are then used either in repo transactions or to back the issuance of ABCPs. Finally, MMMFs buy ABCPs or engage in repos and issue shares that constitute inside money.

Shadow banking—and unregulated banking in general—is highly procyclical. In good times, prices for shadow banking products are stable. Someone is always willing to buy ABSs or CDOs, as one can use them as collateral in a repo to obtain liquidity whenever needed. Price stability makes repo lenders comfortable with requesting lower haircuts. Repo haircuts for many securities fell to 0% during the shadow banking boom. We have noted that repo haircuts play a similar role in the shadow banking sector, as do reserve requirements in traditional banking. Lower haircuts allow more inside money to be created, which, ultimately, fuels the economic boom further.

As we have just discussed, under Basel II, effective capital requirements become less restrictive over the course of an economic boom. Stable prices of shadow banking products, for instance, prompt banks' internal risk systems to indicate lower credit risk. Banks can then extend more credit with the same amount of equity.

Since trustworthy borrowers have already obtained loans, banks lower their lending standards in order to find new borrowers.[22] By repackaging these loans in opaque shadow banking securities such as CDOs and CDO^2, which have been systematically overrated by rating agencies, shadow banking succeeds to transform even high-risk loans into inside money.[23]

While inside money expands and credit is granted on generous levels, the real economy is flourishing. Everyone who wants to own a house, buy a car, or take up a student loan can do so. And a lot of people want to do so. People buy houses not only to live in but also to speculate on rising prices. The speculative demand drives real estate prices further up. Rising prices of real estate property, which is used as collateral in mortgage loans, indicates lower credit risk in banks' internal risk-management systems. Further, rising prices of real estate property positively affect the rating agencies' credit rating of mortgage-backed securities (MBSs), a subset of ABSs that are backed by mortgage loans. As we know by now, both effects allow for more inside money to be created.

Leads to a Shadow Banking Panic ...

Every financial bubble eventually bursts. The U.S. housing bubble burst in 2007 when subprime mortgage borrowers started to default.[24] If borrowers whose mortgage loans were structured into an MBS default, the price of these MBSs falls. So do prices of all CDO structures that are linked to the defaulting borrowers. Increasing default rates led to a decline in the prices of MBSs, and CDOs of MBSs, and CDO^2 of CDOs of MBSs, and CDO^3 of CDO^2 of CDOs of MBSs. Increasing default rates on mortgages led to a spike in foreclosure rates and an increase in vacant housing units. In turn, the supply overhang on the real estate market led to a decrease in house prices. Since real estate property is used as collateral in mortgage loans, the decline in house prices caused many previously fully secured mortgages to go under water. Consequently, prices of MBSs dropped further, as the collateral no longer protected investors from credit risk.[25]

Repo lenders started to realize that MBSs were more risky than they appeared to be during the shadow banking boom. In turn, they raised haircuts. Repo borrowers could obtain less money by pledging MBSs as collateral. To compensate for the lost funding sources, repo borrowers had to sell MBSs, further accelerating the fall in prices. A downward spiral characterized by declining collateral prices, rising haircuts, and fire sales of assets started to pick up pace.[26]

During the early days of the financial crisis of 2007–08, many experts remained confident that non-subprime mortgage markets would remain unaffected.[27] They were wrong. The crisis escalated into a panic that gripped the whole financial system. Financial institutions that lost their short-term funding sources had to sell assets on a large scale. The downward spiral of falling prices spilled over to ABSs that were unrelated to subprime mortgages. By the second half of 2007, the panic had already infected large parts of the shadow banking sector. Suddenly, financial institutions tried to get rid of all sorts of shadow banking products.[28]

Eventually, traditional banks started to face serious problems as well. Repo financing was a major channel for banks to finance their assets. When repo financing dried out due to rising haircuts and decreasing collateral prices, banks had difficulty finding alternative financing sources.

To make things worse, banks came under pressure from their ABCP commitments. Recall that banks provided credit and liquidity guarantees to ABCP conduits that were backed by ABSs. Due to the deteriorating market conditions for ABSs, investors lost their confidence in ABCPs and started to sell them. Sponsoring banks were forced to inject vast amounts of money into the respective ABCP conduits to honor their insurance promises.[29]

For the first time in the digital age, banking entered full-blown panic mode. The financial crisis of 2007–08 is sometimes referred to as the *silent bank run*.[30] In contrast to earlier banking panics, nobody was lining up in front of banks. The panic spread among money market participants, in particular, banks, MMMFs, hedge funds, and large investors. As repo lenders or ABCP buyers, they withdrew their money electronically by discontinuing rolling over short-term credit.

The consequences of the shadow banking panic, however, were identical to earlier banking panics. A credit crunch followed suit, as companies were no longer able to obtain loans.[31] Inside money was destroyed on a large scale, leading to a sharp monetary contraction and a looming threat of deflation.[32]

... and a Large-Scale Bailout

With the panic starting to threaten the functionality of the financial system, the Fed stepped in as a lender of last resort. The Fed replaced the dried-up liquidity previously provided by shadow banking. It lowered its target for the federal funds rate.[33] In addition, the Fed started to lend directly to financial institutions in the shadow banking sector, particularly to broker-dealers such as investment banks. It also extended the maturity of its loans; banks were now allowed to borrow from the Fed for up to 90 days. Furthermore, the collateral standards for the above-mentioned loan facilities were lowered.[34]

These measures addressed liquidity problems in both traditional and shadow banking, but the panic had already escalated beyond a pure liquidity crisis. The rapid price collapse of ABSs, MBSs, and CDOs hit banks hard, as they kept the most vulnerable tranches of these securities on their books. They suffered staggering losses.[35] At this time, banks were operating with razor-thin equity buffers, as they were so successful in minimizing Basel II capital requirements. The threat of insolvency was suddenly looming over many banks. Bear Stearns was one of the first large banks to fail, and regulators organized a merger with J.P. Morgan to avoid a further escalation of the panic.[36]

Soon after the problem with Bear Stearns was "solved," another large bank started to stumble: Lehman Brothers. Contrary to Bear Stearns, regulators decided to let Lehman fail. The bankruptcy of Lehman Brothers was a historic turning point. Before the bankruptcy of Lehman, it was beyond imagination that a large investment bank would be unable to fulfill its contractual obligations. After the bankruptcy of Lehman, people suddenly lost trust in all banks.[37]

This had far-reaching consequences for shadow banking, as banks had sponsored many entities and issued credit and liquidity guarantees to ABCP conduits. MMMFs quickly attracted attention because some of them were holding ABCPs with credit and liquidity insurance from Lehman. No one knew exactly which MMMFs were exposed to Lehman. As a result, money market investors started to panic and ran MMMFs.

In turn, the government had to guarantee all liabilities of MMMFs. This emergency measure was taken despite MMMFs being explicitly carved out from deposit insurance. In addition, the Fed injected further liquidity into the financial system to stop the run on MMMFs. Banking guarantees started to expand to shadow banking: Financial institutions other than banks got access to the lender of last resort, and MMMF shares—the deposits of shadow banking—received full government guarantees.[38]

Because of the catastrophic events triggered by the bankruptcy of Lehman Brothers, regulators did not dare letting any other large bank fail. The government launched the Troubled Asset Relief Program (TARP). This program allowed the Treasury to buy both bank equity and shadow banking products. By directly buying ABSs and MBSs, prices could be stabilized, and the shadow banking panic was finally brought to a halt.[39]

The policy measures taken during the financial crisis of 2007–08 were necessary. They prevented a complete collapse of the financial system, which would have ended in disaster. Despite the policy actions taken, the financial crisis still triggered a severe recession, which is now sometimes called the *Great Recession*. Income fell, and unemployment increased dramatically.

In addition, the policy measures themselves came at significant costs. Government debt, for instance, spiked. Such direct costs have been discussed in great detail. The indirect costs are, however, more fundamental. The massive expansion of government guarantees will likely shape our financial system for decades to come.

——— NOTES ———

1. Financial innovation was, for example, considered to be one of the reasons for the decline in output volatility—the so-called *great moderation* (Dynan, Elmendorf & Sichel, 2006). An overwhelming majority in the economic discussion perceived financial innovation as a stabilizing factor for the financial system and did not raise material concerns. A notable exception was Rajan (2006), who took a more cautious view and called for regulatory responses to financial innovation.

2. See, for example, Greenspan (1998).

3. Basel II is organized along three pillars. We focus on the first pillar, which is intended to restore the effectiveness of risk-weighted capital requirements. For the original document, see Basel Committee on Banking Supervision (2004).

4. See Haldane and Madouros (2012). The complexity of banking and banking regulation puts high costs on society, since highly skilled people devising and running risk-management systems could perform other productive tasks in the economy.

5. Bair (2007).

6. Basel Committee on Banking Supervision (2006, 1).

7. French (2004). In fact, the United States did only adopt Basel II for large global banks, as regulators had strong reservations against full implementation.

8. The development of photocopy machines have moved things along. Rating agencies started to face the problem that paying investors could copy rating manuals and distribute copies to associated investors (see White 2010).

9. See Hill (2004).

10. See White (2010).

11. Moody's Corporation, for instance, was earning more with rating structured finance products (44% of its revenues) than with rating corporate bonds (32%) in 2006 (Coval, Jurek, and Stafford 2009, 4–5).

12. Excerpts of emails published in the report of the U.S. Securities and Exchange Commission (2008) epitomize the business practices of rating shadow banking products. One excerpt says, for example: "One analyst expressed concern that her firm's model did not capture 'half' of the deal's risk, but that 'it could be structured by cows and we would rate it.' [Email No. 1: Analytical Staff to Analytical Staff (Apr. 5, 2007, 3:56 pm).]" (p. 12).

13. See Hill (2009). Structures such as CDOs and CDO^2 are good examples of this practice. An accurate rating of these products is very difficult. The underlying assets are thousands of loans. All of these loans are possibly correlated in their probability of default. The probability of default of mortgages taken by homeowners living in the same city, for example, are correlated: If a large local employer goes bankrupt, it is likely that not one but many homeowners will run into troubles. Accounting for these interdependencies in a credit rating is hard, if not impossible. As an analytical manager at a rating agency remarked on the CDO market: "Let's hope we are all wealthy and retired by the time this house of cards falters" (U.S. Securities and Exchange Commission 2008, 12).

14. According to Scholtes and Beales (2007), more than 37,000 structured finance products had been awarded with a top rating AAA shortly before the crisis. In contrast, only five nonfinancial U.S. companies obtained top ratings. Many of these AAA-structured finance products were downgraded by several notches during the financial crisis of 2007–08. Benmelech and Dlugosz (2010) show that shadow banking products were systematically overrated.

15. See the disclaimer of Standard & Poor's on http://www.standardandpoors.com/regulatory-affairs/ratings/en/us.

16. Both statistics have been taken from Nersisyan and Wray (2010, 10–11).

17. See also Rosenberg and Given (1987).

18. See Basel Committee on Banking Supervision (2006).

19. The microeconomic approach to banking regulation has recently come under pressure. See, for example, Hanson, Kashyap, and Stein (2011) and Brunnermeier et al. (2009), who call for a macroprudential approach.

20. See Basel Committee on Banking Supervision (2004).

21. For a discussion of the procyclicality of capital requirements, see, among others, Blum and Hellwig (1995), Danielsson et al. (2001), Kashyap and Stein (2004), and Repullo and Suarez (2013).

22. See Demyanyk and Van Hemert (2011) for empirical evidence on the deteriorating quality of loans in the run up to the crisis.

23. One important reason was the insurance of some shadow banking products provided by financial companies such as American Insurance Group (AIG); see, for example, Mehrling (2011). For ease of presentation, we have refrained from including this feature in the narrative of the shadow banking panic. However, we will touch on it when looking at today's derivative markets in the next chapter.

24. This is the reason the financial crisis of 2007–08 is sometimes called the *subprime mortgage crisis*. Subprime mortgage borrowers are characterized by low creditworthiness—that is, lending to subprime borrowers comes with high credit risk.

25. Rating agencies' risk models did not anticipate any of these chain effects. None assumed declining house prices, and if they did, credit risk measures based on these models exploded. See Coval, Jurek, and Erik Stafford (2009).

26. See Gorton and Metrick (2012).

27. In 2007, Fed Chairman Bernanke (2007) said that "we see no serious broader spillover to banks or thrift institutions from the problems in the subprime market; the troubled lenders, for the most part, have not been institutions with federally insured deposits." Henry Paulson, then secretary of the Treasury Department, thought that the troubles on the subprime mortgage market were "largely contained" ("Treasury's Paulson" 2007).

28. In the second half of 2007, for instance, repo lenders started to ask for higher haircuts on securities unrelated to the subprime mortgage crisis; see Gorton and Metrick (2010).

29. See Brunnermeier (2009).

30. "Silent bank run" is from Brunnermeier (2009, 90). Gorton and Metrick (2012) coined the term "run on repo."

31. See Ivashina and Scharfstein (2010) for empirical evidence.

32. The Board of Governors of the Federal Reserve (2009) noted that "inflation could persist for a time below rates that best foster economic growth and price stability in the longer term."

33. The *federal funds rate* is the interest rate at which banks lend federal funds, that is, outside money, to each other. Lending on the federal funds market is usually overnight and uncollateralized. Commercial banks can lend directly from the Fed at the so-called discount window, which has rates slightly above the targeted federal funds rate. We discuss the role of the federal funds rate in great detail in the next chapter.

34. For a short overview over the various ad hoc policy measures of the Fed during the panic, see Bernanke (2009).

35. See Gorton (2010), who compiled a chronology of the major events of the crisis. Banks announced hundreds of billions of dollars of losses in 2007 and 2008.

36. See Brunnermeier (2009) and Orticelli (2009). When Bear Stearns ran into trouble in March 2008, it "had about 150 million trades spread across various counterparties." (Brunnermeier 2009, 88). To prevent a global financial meltdown, it was thought necessary that Bear Stearns live up to its contractual promises. In turn, the regulators decided to avoid bankruptcy. This was the reason they sweetened the takeover of Bear Stearns by another investment bank, J.P. Morgan, with a nonrecourse loan of $30 billion against Bear Stearns's assets. J.P. Morgan had little downside risk in taking

over Bear Stearns, given the support of the Fed. In the name of financial stability, the Fed put a lot of taxpayers' money at risk.

37. It appeared the government was unable to motivate other banks to take over Lehman at acceptable terms. Furthermore, the political will seemed missing to bail out the bank. Henry Paulson said after Lehman's fall that he "never once considered it appropriate to put taxpayer money on the line in resolving Lehman Brothers" (van Duyn, Brewster, and Tett 2008).

38. See Baba, McCauley, and Ramaswamy (2009). Because inside money created in the shadow banking sector is in the form of traded securities, the lender-of-last-resort role of government manifests itself differently. Mehrling (2011) uses the phrase "dealer of last resort" to describe the new role the central bank has taken to deal with the financial crisis of 2007–08.

39. Massad (2011) describes the specific actions that were taken by the government and the Fed. First, the government provided the banks with equity to prevent bankruptcy. Second, the government bought shadow banking products to stabilize prices in these markets.

<u>7</u> The Financial System after 2008

The large-scale bailout worsened the already dysfunctional state of our financial system. The most disturbing regulatory development is the expansion of government guarantees without accompanying effective regulation. Historically, guarantees were only supposed to apply to deposits of banks. The financial crisis of 2007–08, however, forced regulators to take on a much broader role.

Banking Is Out of Control

Governments and central banks expanded the scope of banking guarantees in two dimensions. First, the guarantees were extended to financial institutions in the shadow banking sector. Just as governments guaranteed inside money created by traditional banking in the first half of the 20th century, they now guarantee inside money created by shadow banking. Second, the guarantees became all-encompassing for large banks. Large banks enjoy, de facto, full protection from insolvency. After Lehman, the bankruptcy of another large financial institution became inconceivable. Such institutions are often called *too big to fail*.[1]

Too-Big-To-Fail Institutions Dominate the Financial System

The expression *too big to fail* became widely known after the FDIC rescued Continental Illinois National Bank and Trust Company in

1984.[2] Financial institutions are considered too big to fail if they cannot go bankrupt without triggering massive turmoil in the financial markets. Such a threat deters regulators from forcing a too-big-to-fail institution into bankruptcy. More than 20 years after the rescue of Continental Illinois, the failure of Lehman Brothers forcefully confirmed the existence of the too-big-to-fail issue.

A too-big-to-fail institution enjoys guarantees on all liabilities, not just deposits. Market participants are thus willing to lend money to too-big-to-fail institutions at lower risk premiums. They know their investment is ultimately guaranteed by the government. Lower risk premiums translate into lower funding costs. And lower costs translate into higher profits. We should see these guarantees as what they are: a subsidy for large banks.

We have discussed how current regulations favor large banks. The too-big-to-fail subsidy provides even more of an incentive for banks to become large. Some have estimated an implicit subsidy of $700 billion per year for the 29 most systemically important banks in the world.[3] To put this number into perspective: Every human being on this planet hands over $100 to these large banks every year.

Extending guarantees to all liabilities of too-big-to-fail institutions exacerbates moral hazard problems.[4] Provided with cheap funding no matter what, lenders have no incentive to monitor too-big-to-fail institutions and to prevent them from taking excessive risks. The longer we live with too-big-to-fail institutions, the more accustomed we become with the notion that all of their liabilities are guaranteed by governments. This situation is analogous to the one with deposit insurance described earlier. Similar to perceiving deposits as risk-free today, we will perceive all forms of debt of too-big-to-fail institutions as (counterparty) risk-free at some point.

Regulators Fail to Restrict Too-Big-To-Fail Institutions

Faced with this situation, regulators did what they have done before. They started to devise and implement more banking regulation. Regulators once more chose capital requirements as their regulatory tool of choice. They updated capital requirements and hoped to discourage too-big-to-fail institutions from taking excessive risks.

The new international effort to fix banking regulation is called Basel III, and it is as doomed to fail as its predecessors were. Basel III barely addresses any of the fundamental problems that we identified earlier. It still builds on internal risk-management models for risk weighting.[5] Capital requirements continue to be ridiculously low.[6] In addition, Basel III further increases the complexity of banking regulation.[7] Finally, shadow banking remains largely untouched; the rules still focus on banks, not on banking.

Some economists who are disappointed with Basel III have argued for a radical increase in capital requirements. Admati and Hellwig gained broad attention with a vociferous call for drastic increases in capital requirements. They propose abandoning sophisticated risk weighting measures and implementing capital requirements of 20% to 30%. Equity ratios of banks were within this range before lender-of-last-resort policies and deposit insurance schemes were implemented.[8]

Unfortunately, Admati and Hellwig fail to differentiate between banks and banking. They do not offer convincing solutions to the boundary problem. Banks will react to higher capital requirements as they did before. They will migrate banking into the shadows. Furthermore, new financial insitutions will emerge that will create inside money in an obscure way such that they will avoid the high capital requirements proposed by Admati and Hellwig.[9]

The financial crisis of 2007–08 has proven that an unregulated banking sector can quickly create enough inside money to become systemically relevant. With systemic relevance comes implicit government guarantees and, hence, lower financing costs. This will give unregulated institutions a strong competitive edge over banks, which have to meet the high capital requirements proposed by Admati and Hellwig. At the same time, the systemic relevance will make a bailout necessary in case things turn out bad. We will end up exactly where we are now.

Capital requirements have been the standard response of many economists and politicians. They still want to accompany the carrot of government guarantees with the stick of capital requirements. But over the last 40 years, information technology has turned the stick into a toothpick. Capital requirements no longer work in the digital age.

Institutions that have their liabilities guaranteed by the government will always find ways to circumvent regulation such as capital requirements. It is just too profitable to take excessive risks when your downside is capped. Let us provide you with one example of excessive risk taking that has been fueled by the widespread guarantees for too-big-to-fail institutions: derivatives.

Excessive Risk Taking on the $700 Trillion Derivative Market

Derivatives are as old as financial markets, and many of them serve useful purposes. The defining feature of a *derivative* is that it derives its value from an underlying asset. Corn futures, for example, derive their value from the price of corn.[10] We do not want to dive into an extensive discussion of derivatives. Instead, we want to highlight the crucial relationship between derivatives and too-big-to-fail institutions.

Too-big-to-fail institutions can use derivatives to pursue *tail-risk strategies*. A *tail risk* is supposed to be very unlikely — that is, it lies in the tails of the underlying probability distribution. Such strategies yield positive returns in normal times at the expense of huge losses in case of a tail event.[11]

With tail-risk strategies and government guarantees in place, traders, managers, and bank owners receive the positive returns in good times, whereas government has to enter the scene if things turn out bad. Hence, taxpayers eventually shoulder the huge tail-event loss. Derivative tail-risk strategies contributed to the stellar banking profits during the "golden age of finance" between 1990 and 2007.[12]

American Insurance Group (AIG), a large insurance company, is a well-known example of a company having pursued a tail-risk strategy using derivatives. AIG sold a type of derivative called a *credit default swap* (CDS). A CDS insures against the default of a particular security. The CDSs issued by AIG insured holders of CDOs, in particular, CDOs having subprime MBSs as underlying securities. Such a CDS pays out the resulting loss should the underlying CDO default. Remember that the CDO is itself created out of MBSs, which have again bundled countless mortgages together. In short, such a CDS issued by AIG ultimately derived its value from the ability of thousands of homeowners to service their mortgage loans.

AIG insured a notional amount of more than $500 billion of subprime mortgage securities in the wake of the financial crisis of 2007–08. The tail-risk strategy was very simple: Sell insurance and cross your fingers that you will never have to deliver on your promise. When the tail event occurred—the financial crisis of 2007–08—AIG went bankrupt within one year. The equity was insufficient to cover all the losses incurred. After the experience with the collapse of Lehman, the government stepped in and bailed out AIG to prevent further stress on financial markets. AIG received almost $200 billion of temporary government support.[13]

The example of AIG demonstrates the basic principles of derivative tail-risk strategies. AIG was only able to deliver on its promise because the U.S. government stepped in. Buyers bought derivatives from AIG knowing that the government would ultimately get involved if AIG faced serious trouble. Implicit government guarantees allowed derivative market participants to largely ignore counterparty risk.[14]

Counterparty risk is the possibility of a counterparty in a contract going bankrupt and thus not being able to fulfill its obligation; it is a form of credit risk. Most derivatives feature counterparty risk. If the seller of a derivative goes bankrupt, the derivative becomes worthless.[15]

To mitigate counterparty risk, buyers request collateral from sellers. Both buyer and seller agree on how to value the derivative contract on an ongoing basis. Then, the seller—for example, AIG—posts the corresponding collateral. If the seller defaults, the derivative transaction is unwound at the agreed-on value, and the buyer can sell the collateral to get her money.[16]

It thus seems that counterparty risk should not be much of an issue in derivatives trading and that government guarantees were of no significance. This is not the case. Even by calculating the market value daily and posting collateral accordingly, the buyer can never eliminate counterparty risk completely.

An example clarifies this. Assume that you hold a CDO. To be insured against losses, you buy a CDS on your CDO. This CDS is collateralized by some security. Suppose the seller of your CDS protection defaulted. At this moment, you receive the collateral, but you still own the original CDO. Since you wanted to be protected before, you are not happy with holding the collateral instead of the protection. So you try to find someone else who will sell you a CDS. But as the initial CDS issuer was likely a large financial institution, its failure will cause stress on the whole financial system. Such a situation makes it very difficult, if not impossible, to find a new counterparty that is willing to sell another CDS to you. It is not possible to remove this sort of systemic counterparty risk—that is, replacement risk—with collateral. Only government guarantees completely eliminate it.[17]

Most institutions selling derivatives are too big to fail. The banks who bought CDSs from AIG knew that the government would step in if AIG ran into trouble. They did not worry too much about counterparty risk. If market participants had to take into account the systemic part of counterparty risk, many derivatives would no longer be attractive.

At the moment, there are derivatives not only for credit default protection but also for interest rates, currencies, commodities, and equity shares. The outstanding notional amount of derivatives at the end of 2013 was estimated to be $710 trillion.[18] This is more than 10 times the global gross domestic product (GDP)—that is, more than the value of all final goods and services produced over 10 years on our planet. The outstanding notional amount of derivatives has multiplied several times since 2000. Eventually, another derivative counterparty will have to be bailed out. Considering the fact that AIG only had $500 billion notional amount of CDSs outstanding—which is less than 0.1% of the total outstanding notional amount of derivatives—the next bailout could dwarf any bailout we have seen so far.

With government guaranteeing all liabilities of too-big-to-fail institutions, the stage has been set for a huge derivatives' market. Massively extended government guarantees provide an incentive for excessive risk taking, while banking regulation fails to effectively restrict banking institutions from taking these risks. Banking is out of control.

Central Banks Are Losing Control

While banking got out of control, central banks were losing control. Central banks increasingly struggle with banking in the digital age. Their conventional tools to conduct monetary policy were designed in the industrial age, when traditional banking dominated. The rise of shadow banking has undermined the efficacy of conventional monetary policy.

Conventional Monetary Policy and Shadow Banking

In a banking system, money is first and foremost inside money. The supply of both outside and inside money affects the price level. As such, monetary policy, which is concerned with price stability, is mainly about influencing inside money creation. Central banks cannot directly control inside money creation. They have to use tools that exert influence on inside money creation via *monetary transmission channels*.[19]

Conventional monetary policy is closely tied to banks and their demand for central bank reserves. Banks hold a fraction of their assets in central bank reserves to meet depositors' withdrawal requests, settle payments with other banks, and fulfill legal reserve requirements. The central bank influences inside money creation by changing the amount of available central bank reserves. If it buys government securities against central bank reserves in open market operations, it increases the amount of available reserves, and vice versa.[20]

On the *federal funds market*, banks lend central bank reserves to each other overnight. The *federal funds rate* is the interest rate banks charge each other for lending central bank reserves. If the central bank increases the amount of available reserves, the federal funds rate tends to fall. Likewise, if the central bank decreases available reserves, the federal funds rate tends to rise. The Fed announces a target for the federal funds rate and conducts its open market operations accordingly.[21]

The federal funds rate, however, has no direct effect on shadow banking. In the run up to the financial crisis of 2007–08, inside money created within the shadow banking sector has significantly contributed to the money supply.[22] Key determinants of inside money creation within the shadow banking sector are, among others, asset prices, asset price volatility, collateral quality, and repo haircuts. Open market operations and other conventional monetary policy tools have no direct impact on these determinants. With the digital revolution, conventional monetary policy lost much of its previous influence on inside money creation.[23]

Central banks were unable to counter the unsustainable shadow banking boom. The steady increase of the target for the federal funds rate from 1% in 2004 to 5% at the beginning of 2007 did not curb lending activity in the shadow banking sector. The Fed could not dampen the massive expansion of inside money.[24] Neither could the Fed prevent the drastic contraction of inside money when the crisis finally hit. The federal funds rate was lowered until it hit its lower bound of 0% in 2009. By hitting the so-called zero lower bound, the difficulties for central banks to conduct monetary policy increased further.

The Zero Lower Bound

Central banks cannot induce a federal funds rate below 0%. Recall that the federal funds rate is the interest banks charge when lending reserves to each other. If the federal funds rate were negative, a bank that would lend central bank reserves today would receive back less of it tomorrow. In turn, banks would start hoarding central bank reserves and stop lending them. To prevent such behavior, the central bank would need to charge banks' negative interest on their reserve holdings. If it did so, however, banks could exchange the reserves into cash. Since cash does not feature a negative interest, banks would stop holding central bank reserves and instead just hold cash. Cash—that is, physical currency—implies a *zero lower bound on nominal interest* rates.[25]

With the federal funds rate at zero, banks can obtain central bank reserves on the federal funds market without paying interest for them. Banks are no longer liquidity constrained, and legal reserve requirements are no longer restricting them in granting loans and creating money. Still, they refrain from doing so.

In the aftermath of the financial crisis of 2007–08, it was not the availability of central bank reserves that inhibited inside money creation. Remember that banks are not only restricted in their ability to create money by legal reserve requirements on the asset side of their balance sheet, but also by capital requirements on the liability side. The crisis had destroyed much of banks' equity. To restore their equity after the crisis, banks had to reduce lending activities and deleverage—that is, contract their balance sheets.

Although the Fed lowered its target for the federal funds rate to 0%, traditional banks continued to deleverage and did not offset the drop in inside money previously provided by shadow banking. The *money supply*, which is both outside and inside money taken together, decreased during and after the financial crisis of 2007–08. Conventional monetary policy was exhausted.

The situation in which conventional monetary policy fails to stimulate lending at the zero lower bound is sometimes called a *liquidity trap*. The situation can become worse if prices start to fall, that is, with deflation. Holding outside money yields a positive real return when prices fall. Even if people hoard money, they are able to buy more goods and services with the hoarded money in the future than today. Hoarding money curbs both credit and spending. Inside money creation is inhibited and deflationary tendencies are fostered.

Unconventional Monetary Policy

The economy could have entered a deflationary spiral similar to that of the Great Depression if central banks had restricted themselves to conventional monetary policy. Central banks were well aware of this threat and quickly resorted to unconventional monetary policy tools when the crisis started to escalate. The Fed, for instance, tried to replace the evaporated inside money by increasing the amount of outside money. Recall that in a fiat monetary regime, central banks can create outside money at their discretion. After the financial crisis of 2007–08, the Fed bought large amounts of shadow banking products and government debt with newly created central bank reserves. This course of action is called *quantitative easing*.

On the one hand, unconventional monetary policy measures—such as quantitative easing—prevented the economy from falling into a deflationary spiral. On the other hand, central banks' balance sheets expanded to unprecedented levels. The Fed's balance sheet, for instance, expanded from $0.9 trillion in September 2008 to $2.2 trillion in November 2008. By the end of 2013, six years after the crisis started, the Fed is in the third round of quantitative easing, and its balance sheet has further grown to $4 trillion.[26]

The amount of outside money has more than tripled since 2007. Central banks all over the world have broadened their activities and increased the size of their balance sheets. While deflation was avoided, these drastic measures did not kick-start lending or revive inside money creation. They have only allowed for a sluggish recovery so far.

Contrary to conventional monetary policy, unconventional monetary policy induced central banks to buy and hold privately issued credit. By buying assets on such a large scale, central banks affect prices; that is, they exert considerable influence on the distribution of wealth in the economy. The large-scale purchase of MBSs, for example, creates an upward push on their prices. In this case, holders of MBSs were the beneficiaries of the central bank intervention.[27]

Central banks have also bought substantial amounts of government debt to lower interest rates. While central banks officially targeted an increase in the money supply with these purchases, they also helped governments finance their deficits. Unconventional monetary policy has blurred the distinction between monetary policy and fiscal policy.[28]

Politicization of Central Banks

Although the distinction between fiscal and monetary policy could be dismissed as an issue of interest for academics only, in reality it is not. How a central bank allocates its resources has redistributive effects, both within the private sector and between the private and the public sector. The larger the central bank's balance sheet is, the more wealth is redistributed.

Central banks' potential in redistributing wealth and their role in bank bailouts have increased their political power. The public correctly perceives central banks as powerful actors in economic policy. Consequently, central banks have started to attract political pressure. Central banks' increase in power and discretion endangers their independence.[29]

Many governments are running large and unsustainable fiscal deficits to cover bailout costs and absorb the effects of the financial crisis of 2007–08. Politicians increasingly try to influence monetary policy to avoid hard choices such as reducing government spending or hiking taxes. Public deficits together with fading central bank independence within an unconstrained fiat monetary regime carry the risk of inflation. If taken too far, this course of action could lead to a complete breakdown of the financial system.[30]

NOTES

1. Other phrases, such as *too interconnected to fail*, have recently become popular. For us, the important thing is the *to fail* part. As such, we stick to the traditional phrase even though we agree that it is not simply the size of a bank's balance sheet that matters for systemic relevance.

2. See Wall and Peterson (1990).

3. Haldane (2012a, 4). Chart 4 in Haldane (2012a) shows how the problem has grown over recent years. As Noss and Sowerbutts (2012) explain, other methods can lead to substantially lower or higher estimations of the implicit subsidy for too-big-to-fail banks. Nevertheless, they conclude that "despite their differences, all measures point to significant transfers of resources from the government to the banking system" (p. 13). For an early account of the problem, see O'Hara and Shaw (1990).

4. For an empirical study suggesting that large banks took on more risks after the too-big-to-fail doctrine introduced by the rescue of Continental Illinois, see Boyd and Gertler (1993).

5. We want to highlight two recent documents showing how banks continue to "optimize" risk weights under Basel III. First, the staff report on the J. P. Morgan "whale" trades published by the U.S. Senate Permanent Subcommittee on Investigations (2013) revealed internal conversations about how to "trick" out capital requirements. The head of the Chief Investment Office's equity and credit trading operation unit proposed ways to reduce the risk weight of a portfolio by $7 billion with model changes alone (p. 170). The bank partly implemented the analyst's proposals, but made it clear to him

that such sensitive matters should not be put in emails (p. 194–95). See also Pollack (2013), who compiled the most captious excerpts from the staff report. Second, a document of the Basel Committee on Banking Supervision (2013) demonstrated how much leeway banks have in designing their internal risk-management models. It conducted a hypothetical test-portfolio exercise. In essence, the Basel Committee asked 15 banks how they would risk-weight 26 different portfolios. The level of risk-weight variability is immense. For a diversified portfolio, the most conservative bank allocated €34 million of risk-weighted assets, whereas the most aggressive bank only allocated €14 million. For some portfolios, the banks calculated standardized value-at-risk measures that differed from each other by more than a factor of 30.

6. Basel III requires 7% (4.5% minimum plus 2.5% conservation buffer) of common equity on total risk-weighted assets (Basel Committee on Banking Supervision 2011). Banks can still borrow $93 with only $7 equity. With so little skin in the game, excessive risk taking is very attractive. Moreover, considering the skills of risk managers to calculate low-risk weights, effective capital requirements would probably be even lower.

7. See Haldane and Madouros (2012). Basel I fit neatly on 30 pages; Basel II required more than 300 pages; Basel III ended up longer than 600 pages.

8. Admati and Hellwig (2013). For an earlier account, see Admati et al. (2011). As we have seen in Part One, risk weights were introduced for good reasons. Admati and Hellwig (2013) acknowledge this problem and propose applying risk weights on an institutional level. They suggest that "in some cases … it might be appropriate to have particularly high equity requirements because the systemic risks that these institutions' activities create are very large" (pp. 179–80). They do not explain, however, why risk weighting on an institutional level should outperform previously devised risk weightings on the asset level.

9. Admati and Hellwig (2013) call this argument a bugbear created by the banking lobbyists. They argue that the source of the problem is "that regulators and supervisors have been *unwilling* to apply the tools they have had" (p. 225). Put bluntly, this suggests that regulators are unmotivated people who do not care if bankers taking on massive risks. As an aside, even if this was the case, Admati and Hellwig remain silent on why regulators should be more willing to enforce regulation under their proposed capital requirements. We strongly disagree that the boundary problem should be disregarded as a motivational problem of regulators. Financial services are virtual in nature. It is impossible to anticipate all the possible ways financial institutions will find in the future to circumvent capital requirements or to create inside money in new ways.

10. Let us elaborate on the usefulness of a corn future. Assume that you are a farmer growing corn. You do not know what the market price of corn will be at the end of the harvesting season. If prices collapse, you might not be able to pay your bills. To eliminate this uncertainty, you could go to town and find someone with whom you could agree *today* to sell your corn at a predetermined price. But this might be cumbersome. Financial markets offer commodity futures that allow fixing the price for corn today for a trade in the future, thus eliminating your uncertainty.

11. Traders describe tail-risk strategies vividly as "picking up nickels in front of a steamroller." Following Taleb's (2007) book on the impact of the highly improbable, such tail events are sometimes dubbed "black swans."

12. The phrase "golden age of finance" has been used by Crotty (2007), who was puzzled by the fact that financial institutions make such high profits despite intense competition in financial markets. He considered it likely that these stellar profits were the result of excessive risk taking. Crotty predicted that a systemic event would eventually trigger huge losses.

13. See Sjostrom (2009). Some might object that the AIG bailout turned out to be profitable for the taxpayer and that AIG repaid the debt. There are two major problems with this argument. First, the government had to expose itself to a lot of downside risk, and the bailout could have turned out very costly in the end. Second, by saving AIG, the government committed to bail out failing derivative counterparties and, hence, mitigated counterparty risk in this market to a large extent.

14. The most prominent counterparty of AIG on CDS contracts was Goldman Sachs. It was estimated that Goldman Sachs received $13 billion from the initial $90 billion tranche of the AIG bailout. (Arlidge 2009). Treasury Secretary Paulson, who was responsible for the bailout, was the former CEO of Goldman Sachs. In this specific case, it was a former employee of the derivative buyer guaranteeing that the derivative seller could deliver on the derivative contract.

15. For some derivatives, the counterparty risk only exists for the buyer, whereas the seller does not need to worry. Options, for instance, can never have a value below zero, and sellers never have to worry about the financial situation of their buyers. Swaps, on the other hand, expose both parties to counterparty risk.

16. There are generally accepted models—one example is the Black-Scholes model—to value most derivatives. The International Swaps and Derivatives Association developed contractual agreements that define how to unwind a transaction in case of default. Note that not all derivative transactions are collateralized. There are derivatives that involve no safeguard at all for the buyer in case the seller defaults (Singh 2010). Furthermore, many jurisdictions grant special privileges to certain derivative counterparties in bankruptcy procedures (Bliss and Kaufman 2006).

17. This form of counterparty risk is comparable to the situation of buying fire insurance for a house in a town already on fire. To mitigate risk in derivative markets, regulators often call for a central counterparty. Note, however, that central counterparty clearing is no panacea either. Strong movements in the price of the underlying asset can lead to a default of the central counterparty. Such a default exposes its members to replacement risk. See Kress (2011), who explains why systemic risk in derivative markets remains a concern even if central counterparty clearing is mandatory.

18. For statistics on the notional amount of derivatives, see Bank for International Settlement (2014), which publishes semiannual over-the-counter (OTC) derivatives statistics. These numbers only cover OTC derivatives, not exchange-traded derivatives. Consequently, they underestimate the size of the global derivative market.

19. For an overview over the different transmission channels, see, for example, Mishkin (1996).

20. See Board of Governors of the Federal Reserve System (2005, chap. 3) for the key role attached to reserves.

21. See Taylor (2001) for a detailed account on the effects of open market operations on the federal funds market.

22. For the importance of inside money created by shadow banking, see Figure 4.1.

23. See Friedman (1999) who predicted early on that credit extension by nondepository institutions might threaten the central bank's ability to affect prices and interest rates in the economy. The link between the central bank reserves and the overall supply of credit and money has weakened with information technology and the ensuing new forms of banking; see also Friedman (2000). Empirical evidence in support of this argument is provided by Altunbas, Gambacorta, and Marqués-Ibáñez (2009), who show that securitization weakened the monetary transmission mechanisms. See also Estrella (2002), who concluded that securitization might have undermined the ability of monetary policy to influence real output.

24. Greenspan (2009), the chairman of the Federal Reserve from 1987 to 2006, noted that "the Federal Reserve became acutely aware of the disconnect between monetary policy and mortgage rates when the latter failed to respond as expected to the Fed tightening in mid-2004. Moreover, the data show that home mortgage rates had become gradually decoupled from monetary policy even earlier."

25. To be precise, central banks can lower interest rates slightly below 0% because holding cash in the vault is more costly than holding central bank reserves due to storage costs. Indeed, the Swedish and Danish central banks, as well as the European Central Bank, have had set rates below zero at which banks can hold central bank reserves (Anderson and Liu 2013; Jones 2014). But this does not change the fact that a lower bound of interest exists due to the physical nature of cash.

26. See http://www.federalreserve.gov/monetarypolicy/bst_recenttrends.htm.

27. See Krishnamurthy and Vissing-Jorgensen (2011).

28. See, for example, Goodfriend (2011). In 2011, the Fed bought government debt that amounted to 61% of the total new issuance of federal government debt (Goodman 2012). This intervention reduces the interest rate at which the government can finance its deficit; see also Krishnamurthy and Vissing-Jorgensen (2011) and Hannoun and Hofman (2012).

29. See Plosser (2010) and Hannoun and Hofman (2012) for further discussion. In Japan, where unconventional monetary policies were adopted earlier, the central bank's independence has already been debated. For instance, the Japanese prime minister has overtly put pressure on the central bank of Japan (Sieg and Takenaka 2012).

30. See Plosser (2012), who argues that the lack of central bank independence together with large fiscal deficits were historically often a path toward hyperinflation.

PART THREE

A Financial System for the Digital Age

<u>8</u> Banking Is No Longer Needed

Part One of this book was about the merits and problems of banking in the industrial age. In Part Two, we showed how banking got out of control in the digital age. The disruptive effects of information technology on a banking system culminated in the financial crisis of 2007–08. Information technology was the game changer that made the boundary problem insurmountable. But merely pointing out the flaws of the current banking system is not enough. In this part, we change perspective and turn to the new possibilities that the digital revolution has opened up. We deliver on our promise and present a proposal to restore a functioning financial system.

Our proposal is unique because it embraces the digital age. It systematically takes the creative effects of information technology into account, without falling victim to its disruptive ones. Again, note that we will not discuss the transition from the current banking system to the financial system we envision. Before discussing how to get there, we first need to demonstrate that the destination is the right one: a financial system without banking.

What exactly do we mean by a financial system without banking? Recall that banking is the creation of money out of credit. Not all activities undertaken by banks qualify as banking, and banking is not only undertaken by banks. A *financial system without banking* is a financial system without inside money. It does not imply a financial system without financial institutions that provide payment services, advice on investments, and asset management. There will also be financial institutions that process loan applications and offer access to capital markets for companies.

The difference between a financial system with and without banking will materialize on the systemic level. In this chapter, we walk through the banking functions that we considered essential in the industrial age and explain why we no longer need banking. Nowadays, a financial system can bridge the mismatched needs of borrowers and lenders, address information asymmetries, and provide convenient payment services without resorting to banking.

Changing the "wiring" of our financial system barely affects the "interface" — that is, how households and borrowers access financial services. Handling financial affairs without banking will remain as convenient for households and borrowers as it currently is with banking. We illustrate how financial affairs can be handled in a financial system without banking with a stylized example at the end of this chapter.

In the remainder of Part Three, we elaborate on a blueprint for a financial system without banking. In particular, we discuss how we can prevent the reappearance of banking, how we need to change monetary policy in a world without inside money, and how these changes will affect the economy in general. First of all, however, let us start with demonstrating that banking is indeed no longer needed to match borrowers and lenders.

Pooling and Risk Diversification

Remember how lenders and borrowers differ in their needs regarding loan size and credit risk. On the one hand, businesses prefer large loans to finance expensive machinery and equipment for risky activities. Households that save money, on the other hand, cannot provide borrowers with such large loans. In addition, they are usually risk-averse. Households do not want to tie their financial existence to a single borrower.

Banking institutions overcome this mismatch as financial intermediaries. *Financial intermediaries* use an intermediating balance sheet for their activities. Traditional banks, for instance, hold many small-denominated deposits on the liability side and a diversified portfolio of loans on the asset side.

An intermediating balance sheet does not necessarily lead to banking, that is, the creation of money out of credit. For example, *mutual funds* are nonbanking financial intermediaries. They pool savings from many households and hold a diversified portfolio of financial assets. The difference between mutual funds and banks is the structure of the liability side. Banks issue equity and deposits. Mutual funds issue only equity shares, which fluctuate in value and, hence, do not constitute inside money.[1]

Lending can also take place without financial intermediation. We speak of *disintermediated lending* if lenders and borrowers establish direct-credit relationships. Our use of the term *disintermediated lending* differs from that of others who consider securitization as a form of it. Since securitization takes place on one or more intermediating balance sheets, it should not be subsumed under disintermediated lending.[2]

Without an intermediating balance sheet, pooling and risk diversification require both borrowers and lenders to enter into a large number of credit relationships. A particular borrower has to pool savings from numerous lenders to be able to fund large investments, and a particular lender has to lend to numerous borrowers to diversify credit risk.

In the industrial age, only governments, large companies, and institutional investors could participate in disintermediated lending. Governments have issued government bonds, and large companies have issued corporate bonds. *Corporate bonds* are standardized credit contracts that usually promise to repay their notional amount at maturity and regular interest payments in between. Even though only few companies participate in the corporate bond market, it matters. In 2011, its capitalization was 92% of GDP in the United States. This number is larger than the total amount of bank deposits at that time, which was 81% of GDP.[3]

Corporate bonds are usually issued in denominations of $1,000 or even more. Such large denominations make it difficult for the average household to compose a bond portfolio with adequate risk diversification. Disintermediated lending inhibits risk diversification if the denomination of credit contracts is too large.

One constraint for small denominations is given by technology. In the industrial age, large denominations of corporate bonds were useful, as it made a difference whether a payment had to be processed for a thousand or a million different lenders. This is no longer the case. Information technology relaxed the limits on the number of credit relationships a borrower or lender can manage.

In the digital age, credit contracts can be issued with very small denominations. Disintermediated lending can provide for the same risk diversification as financial intermediaries do. The same reasoning applies for pooling; borrowers can maintain a credit relationship with a large number of lenders. Financial intermediation by banking is no longer required for risk diversification and pooling.

Note that disintermediated lending does not require households to become financial experts and spend time managing a portfolio of several thousand credit contracts. Financial institutions will offer financial advice for households and manage financial affairs. At the end of this chapter, we illustrate with an example how the finances of households and businesses can be managed without banking.

Peer-to-peer lending platforms demonstrate that disintermediated lending allows pooling and risk diversification for households and small businesses. Peer-to-peer lending is relatively new and still of minor quantitative relevance, but it is growing strongly. Households can split their savings into tiny amounts and lend it across thousands of borrowers. At the same time, small businesses and individuals can pool funds from thousands of lenders.[4]

Addressing Information Asymmetries and Conflicts of Interest

How can lenders be confident that the borrowers they lent money to actually pay interest and return the full notional amount at maturity? Back in Part One, we identified information asymmetries as a problem arising with credit. Borrowers usually know more than lenders what gives rise to moral hazard. By monitoring borrowers, lenders can mitigate the problems arising from information asymmetries. Lenders using disintermediated lending channels cannot monitor borrowers themselves. Risk diversification would require a lender to monitor thousands of borrowers. Pooling would further require the lender to coordinate monitoring with thousands of other lenders. The coordination effort and free-riding problems among different lenders precludes lenders from individually monitoring borrowers.

As a result, borrowers usually delegate monitoring to a third party, a *delegated monitor*. In the case of peer-to-peer lending, for instance, the lending platform operator acts as the delegated monitor. This operator monitors borrowers and starts to chase them if they fall behind their repayment schedule.[5]

Dealing with Conflicts of Interest in Banking and Disintermediated Lending

Has a delegated monitor such as a peer-to-peer lending platform the right incentives to monitor borrowers properly? A delegated monitor has no skin in the game: The monitor's money is not on the line if the borrower defaults. The lenders take all the losses. A conflict of interest arises between lenders and the delegated monitor, and it is not clear from the outset whether monitoring can indeed be delegated in such a way.[6]

At first glance, the series of events during the financial crisis of 2007–08 seem to confirm concerns regarding delegated monitors that have no "skin in the game." A popular narrative suggests that securitization—that is, banks moving loans from their balance sheet to the balance sheet of an SPV—played a central role in the crisis because it weakened the lending standards of banks. Securitization supposedly allowed banks to offload credit risks, so they no longer had an incentive to carefully monitor borrowers.

This story is intuitive, but flawed. Recall that the main rationale for securitization was regulatory capital arbitrage, not to offload credit risk from banks to unwitting investors. Banks usually kept the riskiest tranches of the SPV on their own balance sheet, and they provided liquidity and credit guarantees to ABCPs holding ABSs. Most credit risk remained with the sponsoring banks, and they suffered heavy losses during the financial crisis of 2007–08. Banks used securitization to circumvent banking regulations. Securitization and lower lending standards exposed banks themselves to credit risk.[7]

The financial crisis of 2007–08 unveiled, however, conflicts of interests on behalf of credit rating agencies. These conflicts of interest materialized in the flawed ratings of shadow banking products. The failure of rating agencies does not, though, undermine the viability of disintermediated lending. As we noted, securitization is not disintermediated lending.

Rating agencies did such a poor job in rating shadow banking products because these products were deliberately designed to be opaque; no one could assess the monitoring standards of the ultimate loans backing these products before it was too late. Rating agencies have systemically overrated complex products such as CDO^2, which ultimately derive their value from thousands of loans to thousands of borrowers. Delegated monitoring in a banking model does not work.[8]

Delegating monitoring in a disintermediated lending model, however, is a different story. It implies that a single loan to a single borrower is rated. Assessing individual credit risk is much easier than assessing the risk of a shadow banking product—both for the delegated monitor and for the lender.

Corporate bonds exemplify this fact. Rating agencies have not been willing to put their reputations at risk by using generous ratings to increase their revenues. Indeed, rating agencies did well over the past century in rating corporate bonds. Corporate bond markets have passed the test of time and apparently work. If disintermediated lending did not work, bond lenders would have lost money for decades and would have abandoned corporate bond markets a long time ago.[9]

While corporate bond markets show that the conflicts of interests with delegated monitors can be successfully addressed, information technology further enhances the viability of disintermediated lending. The digital revolution allows to get an even better grip on the conflict of interest between lenders and delegated monitors. As the name already indicates, *information technology* transforms the way we can handle information asymmetries.

How the Digital Revolution Enhances Monitoring and Mitigates Conflicts of Interest

In the industrial age, monitoring was a personal affair. Credit officers at banks established long-standing relationships with their borrowers and based their lending decisions mainly on *soft information*. They relied on personal interactions with borrowers to assess whether they were trustworthy. Subjective factors such as honesty, competency, or trustworthiness were critical in the credit officers' lending decisions.

Soft information is hard to communicate. It is difficult to objectively describe the perceived feeling of a credit officer about the trustworthiness of a borrower. In contrast, *hard information*—such as income reports or balance sheets—is quantifiable and verifiable. If delegated monitors collect hard information about borrowers to calculate their credit ratings, third parties and lenders will be in a position to assess monitoring standards.[10]

Hard information allows lenders to spot delegated monitors with poor monitoring standards by comparing them with other delegated monitors even before loans have to be repaid. This way, delegated monitors with poor lending standards quickly suffer reputation damage. The conflict of interest between them and lenders is greatly mitigated.[11]

One reason delegated monitoring in corporate bond markets has worked so well is the abundance of hard information. Companies issuing corporate bonds conduct *financial reporting*. They publish periodic income statements and balance sheets. These reports have to be audited from an independent third party. Financial reporting provides hard information. Lenders can assess the performance and the financial health of a company independently. In turn, rating agencies refrained from attaching overoptimistic ratings to companies issuing corporate bonds. They would have quickly suffered reputation damage if they had done so. Financial reporting helped overcome the conflict of interest between bond lenders and rating agencies.

Financial reporting, however, is not feasible for small businesses and individuals. It is too expensive. Sarah operating her coffee roasting business, for instance, cannot afford to regularly publish detailed and audited financial statements. Fortunately, financial reporting is not the only way to produce hard information about credit risks.

In the 1960s, when credit cards became widespread, credit officers at banks started to use credit scoring. *Credit scoring* is the application of statistical methods to a range of quantitative information such as payment history, income statistics, and many more. Credit scoring requires information technology to efficiently collect the data required as input. Moreover, the statistical methods to extract meaningful information about credit risk require computational power that has not been available before the digital revolution.[12]

Credit scoring has proven superior to the relationship-based methods of credit officers.[13] Over time, credit scoring has been applied to all sorts of consumer credit markets, such as car financing or mortgage lending. In the 1990s, banks started to apply credit scoring to small businesses, for which soft information was typically considered most important. Credit scoring applied to small businesses turned out to be a success story, too. With the abundance of hard information, banks are relying less and less on soft information.[14]

Given that hard information is now available for all credit segments from consumer loans to small and large businesses loans, disintermediated lending has become viable for all sorts of borrowers. As with corporate bonds, the increased availability of hard information mitigates the conflict of interest between lenders and delegated monitors. The relationship lending model of traditional banking has lost its special role in addressing information asymmetries in credit.

The digital revolution fosters the viability of disintermediated lending in yet another way. The Internet puts lenders in an even better position to assess and compare delegated monitors. Information about monitoring standards is aggregated, processed, and distributed better and more cost-efficiently than ever before. This greatly enhances the use of hard information to assess the performance of delegated monitors.

Some peer-to-peer lending platforms, for instance, provide data on *ex post* loan performance, the applied credit scoring models, and the inputs used for these models. It is only a matter of time until third parties systematically collect this information and publish detailed statistics on online platforms to compare delegated monitors. Lenders will have convenient access to the latest statistics on how well delegated monitors are doing in monitoring borrowers. A decrease in monitoring standards will quickly spread and damage the reputation of a delegated monitor. The reputation effect has become decisive in the digital age.

What we envision for financial services is already a reality in many other sectors of our economy. Information technology has revolutionized the way we manage information asymmetries. Service providers of any sort are continuously monitored and rated on the Internet. Some online platforms, for instance, have successfully addressed the information asymmetries between previously uninformed travelers and local service providers such as restaurants, hotels, and car rental companies.[15]

Many established business models to overcome information asymmetries have been revised or abandoned with the rise of information technology. In the case of traveling services, both traditional travel agencies and travel guide books have been increasingly displaced by their digital counterparts. Similarly, banks' relationship lending, which was based on soft information, has become outdated. In the digital age, banking has ceased to add special value in addressing information asymmetries and conflicts of interests.

Liquidity Provision and Payment Services

So far, we have not discussed how to replace banks in providing liquidity and payment services. Having a bank deposit has an advantage over holding a corporate bond or a peer-to-peer loan. A depositor can walk to an ATM at any time and convert the deposit into outside money. We called this feature contractual liquidity. Both a corporate bond and a peer-to-peer loan, in contrast, have a fixed maturity. You cannot go to the borrower and demand conversion into money before the maturity date.

The Rise of Market Liquidity

The promise of contractual liquidity is part of the asset transformation with which banks address the mismatch between lenders and borrowers. Lenders desire liquidity to react flexibly should unexpected expenses arise, and borrowers usually prefer long-term loans for their activities. By offering contractual liquidity, banking institutions provide liquidity insurance for lenders while enabling long-term loans for borrowers.

Contractual liquidity, however, can be substituted by market liquidity. Corporate bonds, for instance, have been traded on secondary markets for a long time. Lenders were able to access liquidity by selling the bonds to other potential lenders. Market liquidity prevented lenders in corporate bond markets from being locked into long-term credit relationships.[16]

In the industrial age, market liquidity was an imperfect substitute for contractual liquidity. Information asymmetries between sellers and potential buyers for most forms of credit were large. Sellers usually knew more about the underlying quality of credit contracts. As such, potential buyers were reluctant to trade. In other words, sellers possessed *insider information*. The resulting threat of insider trading prevented the emergence of liquid secondary markets.[17]

With monitoring based on soft information, potential buyers find it hard to assess the quality of a loan offered on a market and must assume that the seller knows more about it. We have just discussed how information technology led to a shift to monitoring based on hard information. This development also enhances liquidity on secondary credit markets because it mitigates the problem of insider trading.

Financial reporting and public disclosure requirements by issuers of corporate bonds, for instance, reduce the probability that some market participants have insider information. Similarly, peer-to-peer platform operators can achieve the same by publicly disclosing credit scoring results and other price relevant information. This enables potential buyers to independently compare the quality of loans on secondary markets. Transparency reduces information asymmetries between sellers and potential buyers on secondary credit markets.[18]

Peer-to-peer platform operators can take further measures to prevent insider trading. They can impose position limits that restrict the exposure one single lender is allowed to have to one single borrower, which lowers the potential gains from trading on insider information. Furthermore, they can technically inhibit lenders from selling specific loans by only allowing the placement of orders for loans with a certain credit risk and maturity profile. With such a setup, a seller cannot determine which individual loans to sell and, hence, is not able to trade on insider information.

Information technology contributes to market liquidity not only by mitigating insider trading, but also by allowing for *virtual marketplaces*. Virtual marketplaces have increased market liquidity for all goods and services, even for highly specific and nonstandardized goods. Let us illustrate this with an example in the nonfinancial world. Imagine that you move into a new apartment. You own a valuable antique Victorian oil lamp, but there is no place for it in your new apartment. What should you do? Well, you could sell it on an online auction website. Your chances are good that you can sell your lamp within a reasonable time period at a fair price.[19]

Now imagine your grandma was in the same situation 50 years ago. Back then, she could not sell it online. Maybe she asked her friends and relatives whether they wished to own a Victorian oil lamp, or she went to a thrift shop nearby. Presumably, the people she could reach over these two channels were not in desperate need for such a specific type of lamp. The market liquidity of Victorian oil lamps was very low, and chances were high that grandma sold the lamp at a far worse price than you would today.

Virtual marketplaces have increased the market liquidity of Victorian oil lamps. Why is this? First, virtual marketplaces do not require simultaneous physical presence of market participants. Participants all over the world can participate in the same virtual marketplace at negligible costs. As such, virtual marketplaces pool more market participants than their physical counterparts. Lower search frictions make it much easier to find interested buyers and sellers for a particular item.[20]

Second, virtual marketplaces increase transparency. Virtual order books show the willingness of market participants to sell and buy, given a certain price. Moreover, virtual marketplaces often implement electronic reporting about the volumes and the prices of previous trades. Ready access to this market information facilitates both the search for a trading counterparty and the pricing process. Transaction costs are reduced, and market liquidity is enhanced further.[21]

While all sorts of goods and services are traded on virtual marketplaces today, financial assets are particularly well suited to be traded on such markets because they are virtual themselves. Unsurprisingly, many financial assets are already traded on virtual marketplaces. Exchange-traded funds (ETFs) are one example, and they feature particularly low transaction costs.[22] Furthermore, while not being traded fully electronically yet, bond markets have adopted features of virtual marketplaces. Strengthening electronic reporting in corporate bond markets, for instance, halved transaction costs to the range of 0.05% to 0.08%.[23]

Most peer-to-peer platform operators have established virtual marketplaces on which lenders can sell peer-to-peer credit contracts before maturity.[24] Other peer-to-peer lending platforms have an agreement with a third party to organize a common virtual marketplace for peer-to-peer loan contracts of different platform operators.[25] At the moment, these markets are tiny and market liquidity is low. With more market participants and higher trading volumes, however, market liquidity is set to reach levels seen on other virtual marketplaces for financial assets.

Payment Systems for the Digital Age

In the digital age, market liquidity has become a viable substitute for contractual liquidity. But banking institutions also offer payment services. Let us be clear about the difference between payment services and liquidity. Liquidity is the ability to convert any asset to outside money. Withdrawing cash from your deposit at an ATM is equivalent to accessing contractual liquidity; selling an asset on a market is equivalent to accessing market liquidity. Payment services, on the other hand, are about transferring money—be it inside or outside money. Transferring money from one deposit to another one is equivalent to using banks' payment services.[26]

We discussed how banks provide an *accounting system of exchange* that allows for payments with simple accounting entries. The virtual nature of inside money was the reason banks could offer such convenient payment services. The accounting system of exchange allowed people to trade goods and services without having to meet physically, a crucial advantage over using cash. Clearing of payments by banks was important in the industrial age.

Nevertheless, the accounting system of exchange is not unique to banking. Recall our example from Part One: Sittah and Nathan made use of convenient payment services provided by a custodian, Bonafides. No banking—that is, the creation of money out of credit—is needed for this. Every custodian can offer payment services to her customers. Indeed, payment services are also provided by nonbanking companies today.[27]

While banking was never necessary for payment services, information technology has brought forth another possibility to make payments conveniently: digital currencies. *Digital currencies* are virtual outside money. As with using banks' accounting system of exchange, using digital currency as a medium of exchange does not require counterparties to meet physically.

Digital currencies are still in their infancy. But they already feature lower transaction costs than today's accounting system of exchange operated by banks. Whether we use traditional payment services offered by nonbanking companies or we use digital currency, the result remains: We do not need banking to operate an efficient payment system.[28]

One last issue remains. Banks combine payment services and contractual liquidity in a convenient way. Depositors can access liquidity and process payments in one simple step, for example, by paying with a debit card. Without banking, it seems that two steps are required. First, one needs to sell credit on secondary markets to obtain money. Second, one needs to transfer money to the recipient. Do we have to sacrifice convenience without banking?

The answer is again no. People will not have to manually sell credit contracts if they need outside money for payments. Nonbanking financial institutions such as peer-to-peer lending platforms will provide trading algorithms.

Trading algorithms automate buying and selling decisions and facilitate the access to market liquidity. As with peer-to-peer lending, trading algorithms have already been used in practice. Investment banks, for instance, use trading algorithms to manage the client order flow in foreign exchange or equity markets.[29]

Handling Financial Affairs without Banking

We argued that the difference between a banking system and a financial system without banking concerns the "wiring" rather than the "interface." We have explained how the wiring can be done in a financial system without banking by using information technology. Let us now convince you that the interface will stay as simple as it is today. To illustrate how little the end of banking would be felt by households and nonfinancial companies, we continue our example with Sarah and her coffee roasting business in the digital age without banking.

Financial Services for Lenders

Let us assume that Sarah has been a successful coffee roaster. She has made decent profits and put some money aside. Instead of having her savings and financial affairs managed by Alex, the banker, she now relies on Jacob, a financial advisor. Jacob does not offer her a deposit, but a custody account as a hub for payments and investments.

As in the old days with Alex, Sarah has an initial meeting with Jacob. They work out an investment plan together that fits Sarah's risk profile. She is rather risk-averse, so Jacob makes sure that most of her savings are invested in financial assets—such as peer-to-peer loans—with low credit risk, short times to maturity, and high market liquidity. In addition, he diversifies her savings and does not invest more than one cent in a single borrower.

Of course, just as was the case when opening a bank deposit before the introduction of government guarantees, investing still bears some risk. The future is never known, and investment projects sometimes turn out badly. A portfolio of credit always fluctuates slightly in value. In particular, Sarah will lose money on her investment in credit contracts if a borrower defaults. But the risk is well diversified and outweighed by the interest she earns.

After the initial meeting, Sarah obtains an account number and a payment card. She can pay money in her account and make payments at shops with her payment card; both feels virtually identical for Sarah as in the old days when she used a bank deposit. In other words, the interface did not change.

The wiring behind, however, has changed. Jacob has developed trading algorithms that support his handling of Sarah's payments and investments. First, trading algorithms automatically invest money according to her investment needs. As soon as Sarah puts money into her custody account, trading algorithms start skimming through financial markets all around the world to identify and act on suitable buying opportunities.

Second, Jacob's trading algorithms allow Sarah to pay with her payment card. As soon as Sarah swipes her card, trading algorithms sell financial assets to raise money for her to pay for her shopping items. Jacob will optimize Sarah's money holdings to her liquidity needs so that for small purchases, it will not be necessary to sell financial assets. The money from Sarah's custody account is then wired to the custody account of the shop owner. All these steps happen within a matter of seconds while the shop owner is bagging Sarah's purchase.

In summary, Jacob makes it attractive for Sarah to invest her money in credit. Sarah carries only low and well-diversified risks, she can earn interest, and she stays flexible when facing unexpected expenses. After paying Jacob for all his services, she will likely enjoy a positive return. Thanks to information technology, credit can flourish without resorting to banking.

In contrast to banking, however, Sarah does not have to fear any losses if Jacob defaults. Back in the old days, Sarah was always worried that Alex would go bankrupt. She knew that in this case, she would suffer losses and lose access to her savings. With Jacob the custodian, things are different. Jacob only safe-keeps Sarah's money and financial assets. Her savings are not affected by a default of Jacob. Jacob has even made provisions that Sarah can immediately access her savings if he can no longer continue his operations.[30]

Financial Services for Borrowers

So far, we have illustrated that the interface for a saving household barely changes without banking. Let us now take the perspective of a borrower. Assume that Sarah wants to expand her coffee roasting business for which she would need a loan. Her first point of reference is again Jacob, her financial advisor. Jacob offers custody, investment, and payment services, but he cannot offer her a loan. Therefore, he forwards Sarah's loan application to several peer-to-peer lending platforms.

Ethan is the operator of one of the peer-to-peer lending platforms that receives Sarah's loan application. Ethan earns a fee for every loan he underwrites and, hence, might have an incentive to turn a blind eye if a borrower is not trustworthy. Over the years, however, his peer-to-peer platform has built a valuable reputation. He is ranked consistently high on the websites that publish statistics on the performance of peer-to-peer lending platforms. This attracts many households who are looking for safe investment opportunities, as well as many creditworthy borrowers who are looking for affordable loans. It is in Ethan's interest to maintain high standards when assessing Sarah's loan application. He will earn more money in the long term if he resists the temptation to give favorable ratings just to raise profits for a little while.

Therefore, Ethan tries to assess the credit risk as accurately as possible. Similarly to credit officers at today's banks, he uses a credit-scoring model that he developed and calibrated over the years.

He feeds the model with the information he received from Sarah's loan application and any further data she provides. The scoring model calculates Sarah's credit risk and estimates the interest rate she has to pay for the loan. Ethan then provides this information as a listing offer to Sarah.

It turns out that Ethan provided the most competitive offer, so Sarah decides to obtain a loan through him. Jacob notifies Ethan about Sarah's decision, and Ethan lists the loan on his platform. Lenders around the world bid for lending money to Sarah. When the auction closes, Ethan's platform invoices the money from the lenders and transfers it to Sarah's custody account at Jacob. Sarah is now ready to expand her business.

Sarah no longer needs banking to obtain a loan. Also in her role as a borrower, Sarah's interface barely changed. She filled out a loan application, handed it in to her point of contact for financial affairs, and received an offer. The wiring, however, was different. Jacob, her point of contact, did not grant the loan, and neither did Ethan. The loan was granted by thousands of lenders. Information asymmetries and conflicts of interests are addressed in a new way.

Our example with Sarah illustrates that, in the digital age, financial affairs can be handled conveniently without banking. Households saving money can earn interest and nonetheless enjoy convenient payment services. Businesses investing money can obtain a loan quickly and with good conditions. Today's convenience of handling financial affairs has nothing to do with banking. It is information technology that allows for a simple and convenient interface.

Since banking got out of control with the digital revolution, getting rid of banking is a big step forward. We will get rid of all the problems described at length in Part Two. Replacing banking is analogous to replacing an old, centralized, and unreliable power grid with a new, decentralized, and resilient one so that we would no longer experience blackouts and excessive transmission losses. Using power would remain as simple as before: Just plug in your device. In this chapter, we demonstrated that the interface stays the same. In Chapter 11, we elaborate on how the new wiring will improve efficiency, stability, and equity.

In the digital age, banking is no longer special. It can be replaced, and a better financial system is conceivable. One is drawn to ask, if banking is superfluous, why does it still prevail?

──────────────── NOTES ────────────────

1. Money market mutual funds (MMMFs) are an exception in that respect, as their fund shares do constitute inside money. MMMFs are, however, part of shadow banking (see Chapter 5).

2. As Rajan (2006) points out, using the term *disintermediation* for securitization is a "misnomer," given the daisy chain of balance sheets that stand between ultimate lenders and borrowers in shadow banking.

3. Both numbers are from Beck, Demirgüç-Kunt, and Levine (2013).

4. In 2014, Lending Club was the largest peer-to-peer lending platform in the world and continues to grow strongly. The volume of underwritten loans per quarter surged from approximately $110 million in the first quarter of 2012 to almost $800 million in the first quarter of 2014. In total, Lending Club has underwritten more than $4 billion of loans (see Lending Club's home page: https://www.lendingclub.com/info/statistics. action). The second largest platform in the United States is Prosper. As of January 2014, Prosper has underwritten more than $1.3 billion of loans, of which more than $350 million were originated in 2013 (see Prosper's home page: https://www.prosper. com/invest/marketplace-performance). In the United Kingdom, Funding Circle, Zopa, and RateSetter have become the largest companies in this rapidly growing market. Together these three platforms have underwritten a credit volume of over £1 billion (approximately $1.7 billion; see http://uk.zopa.com/, https://www.fundingcircle. com/ and http://www.ratesetter.com/). As of 2014, both lenders and borrowers were often getting better interest rates with peer-to-peer lending than if they had chosen a bank (see "Banking without Banks" 2014).

5. While the term *delegated monitor* is also used for banks in the literature, we only use it for the agency that monitors borrowers in the case of disintermediated lending. A delegated monitor finances its operations by charging the lender, the borrower, or both a fee.

6. The problem is not confined to disintermediated lending, but arises also with financial intermediation. It is sometimes called the double moral hazard problem. For an analytical model, see, for example, Holmström and Tirole (1997).

7. See Part Two. See also Jiang, Nelson, and Vytlacil (2014), who show that securitized loans remaining on banks' balance sheets had higher delinquency rates than securitized loans sold to third parties.

8. See Chapter 5.

9. See Benmelech and Dlugosz (2010, 175), whose results suggest that corporate bond ratings are, even when accounting for the financial crisis of 2007–08, "well calibrated to the underlying economic risk of the issuer." Hill (2004, 44) finds that "there is considerable evidence that in the normal course, they [rating agencies] do a good, if not stellar, job."

10. See Petersen (2004) on the distinction between soft and hard information. As Petersen states, hard information is almost always recorded as numbers, and soft information as text. Hard information is easily and objectively comparable; soft information is not. Hard information can be collected without personal contact, but soft information has to be collected personally. Also, hard information is more objective, and the person or organization evaluating the information does not need to be the one who collects it. In contrast, soft information cannot be easily transferred to people who were not involved in its collection.

11. This effect is even present in the case of securitization (see Keys, Seru, and Vig 2012).

12. A prominent example for credit scoring is the FICO score. For an explanation what quantitative information is used to calculate the score, see http://www.myfico.com/ crediteducation/whatsinyourscore.aspx.

13. See Thomas (2000). See also Grove and Meehl (1996) on the strength of formal judgmental methods in general.

14. In the 1990s, small-business lending was still perceived as one area where relationship lending by local banks played an important role (see, e.g., Berger and Udell 2002). Petersen and Rajan (2002), however, observed that banks have increasingly used hard information in deciding to lend to small businesses; relationship lending became less relevant. Later, Berger and Frame (2007) reviewed different studies and concluded that credit scoring led to increased credit availability for small businesses.

15. Many Internet companies either relax information asymmetries as their main line of business (e.g., TripAdvisor and Yelp) or have implemented mechanisms to ease information asymmetries arising with their main line of business (e.g., eBay).

16. This finding contradicts the analysis of Diamond and Dybvig (1983), who conclude that only demand deposits can offer optimal liquidity insurance, while market-traded financial assets cannot. Nevertheless, Diamond and Dybvig's result hinges on stringent assumptions and has been challenged repeatedly; see, for example, Jacklin (1987) and von Thadden (1998).

17. See Akerlof (1970), the seminal paper on market failure because of the presence of asymmetric information.

18. See Dennis and Mullineaux (2000), who showed empirically that a bank loan is more likely to be sold ("syndicated") when more information about the borrower becomes transparent.

19. For instance, you could have posted your lamp on eBay, an electronic marketplace with more than 140 million active buyers in the first quarter of 2014 (eBay Inc. 2014). On July 16, 2013, more than 30 Victorian oil lamps were offered on www.eBay. com. Unsurprisingly, the eBay market in the United Kingdom is even more liquid (www.eBay.co.uk). On the same date, some Victorian oil lamp offers attracted more than 15 bids.

20. See Duffie, Gârleanu, and Pedersen (2005) for an analysis of how a reduction in search frictions can lead to lower bid-ask spreads in OTC markets.

21. See Domowitz (2002) for how electronic marketplaces can reduce trading costs.

22. Chou und Chung (2006) analyzed spreads on ETFs that track the major equity indices, and found spreads in 2001 to be in the range of 0.1%–0.2%.

23. These numbers are from Bessembinder and Maxwell (2008) and Bessembinder, Maxwell, and Venkataraman (2006), who compared corporate bond transaction costs in the United States before and after the introduction of the Transaction Reporting Engine (TRACE).

24. For example, the "Rapid Return" function of Zopa (http://help.zopa.com/customer/ portal/articles/1097445-how-do-i-access-my-money-with-rapid-return-) and the "Sellout" function of RateSetter, which can be found in the FAQs (http://www.ratesetter. com/help/faq.aspx). On Funding Circle you can also sell and buy loan parts (https:// support.fundingcircle.com/forums/21584128-Buying-and-selling-loan-parts).

25. Lending Club and Prosper, for example, work together with Folio Investing. See https://www.lendingclub.com/public/mainAboutTrading.action and https://www. prosper.com/invest/trade-notes/.

26. It is sometimes difficult to separate contractual liquidity and payment services, as banking often combines the two functions. This occurs, for instance, when you buy a coffee and pay with your debit card. If both the person buying the coffee and the shop owner have a deposit at the same bank, payment is made exclusively with inside money. Contractual liquidity is not even tapped. The payment is made by simply shifting inside money from one party to the other (see our example for money creation in traditional banking in Chapter 2). If payments are made between counterparties who do not have accounts at the same banking institution, then outside money in the form of central bank reserves is usually involved. In the case of commercial banks, payments are settled (in a netted fashion) with central bank reserves. In this case, paying for a coffee with a debit card is a combination of accessing contractual liquidity and using banks' payment services. See Hancock and Humphrey (1998) for more information on payment settlements between banks.

27. One modern example of a custodian offering payment services is M-PESA, which allows payments with mobile phones in Kenya. See http://www.safaricom.co.ke/ personal/m-pesa.

28. Research on digital currency is still emerging. Currently, Bitcoin is the best-known digital currency. For more information on Bitcoin, see Nakamoto (2008). For a discussion of Bitcoin, see Barber et al. (2012). In 2014, Bitcoin transaction fees were minimal, sometimes even completely absent, while fees for payments through the banking system—including credit card transactions—were based on single-digit percentage points of the transaction volume (Andreessen 2014).

29. See King and Dagfinn (2010) for the importance of algorithmic trading in foreign exchange markets. See Hendershott, Jones, and Menkveld (2011) for the positive effects of algorithmic trading on liquidity on equity exchanges. As part of the discussions around high-frequency trading, trading algorithms have attracted public criticism. See, for example, Lewis (2014). The major problem with high-frequency trading is not, however, the use of trading algorithms per se, but that some market participants obtain privileged access to client order information from brokers and exchanges. The privileged access allowed them to "front run" orders and earn a risk-free profit at the expense of investors.

30. P2P Finance Association (2013) in the United Kingdom has defined operating principles for its members that include the orderly administration of contracts in the event that a platform ceases to operate.

<u>9</u> Accounting for the Future: End Banking

What we have discussed in the previous chapter is nothing fundamentally new. Many have questioned the need for banking in the digital age. Haldane, for instance, once noted, "The banking middle men may in time become the surplus links in the chain. Where music and publishing have led, finance could follow. An information web, linked by a common language, makes that disintermediated model of finance a more realistic possibility."[1] The time has arrived. Banking is already the surplus link that is no longer needed.

Banking Still Dominates

Just because we no longer need banking, however, does not mean that banking will vanish. Technological progress by itself will not bring the end of banking. Banking is too pervasive because creating money out of credit is so attractive. Holding inside money has one crucial advantage over holding other forms of credit, as described next.

Credit always features some credit and interest rate risk. Borrowers might default, and interest rates might change. Both lead to continuous price fluctuations for nonbanking credit. Even a perfectly diversified portfolio of credit contracts always fluctuates in value. A credit portfolio that is worth $100 today might have a value of $100.10 or $99.90 tomorrow.

In contrast, inside money does not feature price fluctuations. On the one side, inside money is credit and pays interest. On the other side, inside money feels as safe as outside money. Except in times of crises, $100 of inside money today will be worth $100 tomorrow.

We have seen that the absence of price fluctuations does not mean that inside money is risk-free. Banking only transforms risk; it cannot eliminate risk. Banking trades credit and interest-rate risk against liquidity risk. Liquidity risk should better be called banking risk. Banking manages to suppress credit and interest-rate risk during normal times, but at the cost of exposing inside money holders to tail risk: bank runs and banking panics.

Recall that banking panics have devastating effects on the real economy, which forces governments to implement guarantees. While it might be ex ante preferable to adopt a no-bailout policy, the government is forced to overthrow its policy when the banking panic eventually happens. The costs of not intervening during a banking panic are too high. Regardless of prior commitments, governments have always responded to banking panics by insuring banking risk, that is, by guaranteeing the value of inside money.[2]

In a fiat monetary regime, governments can guarantee the nominal value of inside money. If necessary, the government can print outside money and exchange it one-to-one with inside money. The almighty government is, however, an illusion. Governments might fail to guarantee the real value of inside money. They do not control the creation of inside money, and, hence, if too much inside money is created, governments will fail to ensure that $100 of inside money today buys the same amount of goods and services that $100 bought yesterday. The absence of price fluctuations on inside money is an illusion that breaks down with inflation.

Notwithstanding its illusive character, government guarantees still incentivize everyone to participate in banking. It is relatively unattractive to hold nonbanking credit because the guarantees redistribute banking risk from inside money holders to either taxpayers (if bailouts are financed with taxes) or to everyone who is entitled to nominal claims (if bailouts are financed with the printing press).

You have to carry banking risk whether you hold your wealth in inside money or not. This is the externality of banking in the digital age, that is, of unrestricted banking with government guarantees: Virtually no one can escape from banking risk.[3]

As such, everyone is better off to participate in banking. If one is forced to carry banking risk, one can at least enjoy the benefits of inside money. We have already discussed how government guarantees are effectively an implicit funding subsidy for banking. The socialization of banking risk is the flip side of the implicit funding subsidy.

The subsidy for banking and the way the cost of the subsidy is distributed make it hard for nonbanking institutions to compete with banking institutions. Further progress in information technology will not inevitably lead to the end of banking, but only to the reappearance of banking in various new forms.[4] We need a political response to unconstrained banking in the digital age. We have to end banking.

How Not to End Banking

The issues with banking have been known for a long time. We are not the first ones who want to end banking. After the experience with the Great Depression, some economists—including Nobel Prize laureates—have called for ending banking.[5]

Narrow Banking: Revisiting Banks

Narrow banking is the most prominent proposal along these lines. The name is misleading, as narrow banking is actually about ending banking at banks. Proponents demand that banks should no longer be allowed to lend out deposited money. The bank deposit contract would become a safekeeping contract again. Depositors of narrow banks would not earn interest, as their deposits would no longer be used to grant loans to interest-paying borrowers. Banks could only lend money if depositors gave up the contractual liquidity of their deposits and transferred their savings to accounts that they could not readily access. In a nutshell, narrow banking wants to split banking into two separate business lines—the business of lending and the business of safekeeping—to prevent inside money creation.

Various versions of this idea were developed. Fisher's 100% money proposal is probably the best known. It demands that for every dollar in deposits taken, banks must hold one dollar liquidity reserves either in cash or in government debt. Deposits would have to be backed with a 100% liquidity reserve. This ensures that banks would always be able to meet withdrawals from depositors. Banks could no longer create money out of credit, and bank runs could no longer occur.[6]

Many economists criticized narrow banking for curtailed liquidity provision and predicted that it would impair the ability of the financial system to accumulate capital. Narrow banking prohibits banks from offering contractual liquidity. Opponents claim that lenders would react to this inconvenience by holding more of their wealth in cash and narrow deposits instead of savings accounts to remain flexible. In turn, credit availability would be lowered.[7]

The digital revolution took the edge off the liquidity argument. Narrow banking is an idea of the industrial age. Back then, we still needed banking to match borrowers and lenders. Times have changed. We have seen how market liquidity can substitute for contractual liquidity in the digital age.

The second major argument against narrow banking, however, cannot be rebutted. Fisher's 100% money proposal does not consider the boundary problem. It prohibits banks from lending deposits, but it does not prohibit shadow banking institutions from extending credit and transforming it via securitization, repos, and MMMFs into inside money. As we found out the hard way during the financial crisis of 2007–08, banking is an activity that is not confined to the institutions called "banks."[8]

Having not gained much attention for decades, narrow banking was brought back into the public discussion by the financial crisis of 2007–08.[9] *Positive money*, for instance, is a political movement that rediscovered the ideas of narrow banking.[10] Being almost identical to previous narrow banking proposals, its modern counterpart also runs into the boundary problem.

In general, contemporary proponents of narrow banking do not account for how the world has changed with the digital revolution. The idea of narrow banking originated more than 80 years ago, during a time when banking was still a paper-based business. On the one hand, current narrow banking proposals neglect how information technology has worsened the boundary problem. On the other hand, they do not acknowledge the opportunities information technology provides. Notwithstanding our critique, narrow banking proposals such as positive money are moving in the right direction to establish a better financial system. Positive money proponents, for instance, rightly point out that banking is a source for instability and that it extorts tremendous profits for its owners and employees by creating inside money.[11]

Limited Purpose Banking: Revisiting Financial Institutions

Contrary to narrow banking, limited purpose banking takes the boundary problem seriously. Limited purpose banking does so by regulating all financial institutions, not only banks. In essence, limited purpose banking demands that all financial institutions be set up as mutual funds; that is, they have to be fully funded with equity.[12]

Furthermore, financial institutions would only be allowed to invest in credit that has been screened by a regulator or by a rating agency commissioned by the regulator, the Federal Financial Authority (FFA). The FFA would ultimately be responsible for assigning or certifying every credit rating in the economy. Hence, the FFA would become an almost almighty governmental authority that would take full responsibility for monitoring every borrower in the economy.[13]

While limited purpose banking acknowledges the boundary problem, it comes with some serious drawbacks. In particular, limited purpose banking monopolizes monitoring and moves it from the private into the public sphere. Encumbering the government with this task would come at a high price. Competition between delegated monitors would cease to exist and would be replaced by bureaucratic processes governed by law. The lack of healthy competition for monitoring would likely result in inefficiencies and, ultimately, higher costs for both borrowers and lenders.

In addition, centralizing all monitoring in one single institution—be it public or private—needlessly concentrates power. Remember the popular saying (from Lord Acton): power corrupts and absolute power corrupts absolutely. With its key role, the FFA ultimately decides who gets access to credit in the economy, and who does not. Limited purpose banking would establish a governmental monopoly in screening and monitoring, which would ultimately lead to cronyism.[14]

Although limited purpose banking is a step in the right direction to address the boundary problem, it creates an overwhelming public authority. Moreover, it does not solve the boundary problem. Limited purpose banking requires the regulator to differentiate between financial and nonfinancial companies. In large industrial companies, treasury departments conduct operations that cannot be distinguished from financial institutions. They manage their company's liquidity needs and hedge financial risks. Also, small and medium-sized companies grant short-term credit to their customers. Finding clear legal criteria to categorize a company as financial is impossible.

How to End Banking

The boundary problem of financial regulation not only complicates the life of today's banking regulators, it also requires careful attention if one is attempting to end banking. Prohibiting the creation of money out of credit within banks—as in narrow banking—will not succeed in ending banking. Banking will reemerge in institutions not called banks. Putting a stifling regulatory framework around all financial institutions to prevent banking—as in limited purpose banking—does not fully address the boundary problem either. Banking might reemerge in institutions that are called "nonfinancial."

Again, banking is not confined to a certain set of institutions that define themselves as banks or financial institutions. It is not even confined to a single balance sheet. Banking's roots run deeper. Its origins are in double-entry bookkeeping. Ending banking should start at this fundamental level. It should tackle banking at the level of accounting.

Banking as a Particular Application of Financial Techniques

Recall the six financial techniques that can be used to transform credit to inside money: pooling, diversification, structuring, collateralization, insurance, and contractual liquidity.[15] If we outright forbid these techniques, banking would no longer be possible. But let us not overshoot the mark. These financial techniques serve many useful purposes, too.

Households, for instance, invest their savings in a diversified manner, and almost every company funds its activities with equity and debt; that is, it structures the liability side of its balance sheet. In addition, collateralization allows borrowers to obtain loans at lower interest rates and aligns their incentives with those of lenders. Finally, most of us have bought insurance and enjoy the safety it provides.

The purpose of the financial system is to enable a decentralized and capital-intensive economy. All financial activities that facilitate the coordination of economic activities and the accumulation of capital without giving rise to banking are useful. We need to find a way that prohibits the application of financial techniques for banking but allows all useful applications.

For the moment, let us make a provisional distinction between financial and nonfinancial companies. A financial company, such as a bank or a mutual fund, holds mostly financial assets on its balance sheet. In contrast, a nonfinancial company, such as a coffee roasting company, holds mostly nonfinancial assets. Of course, this distinction runs into the boundary problem of financial regulation, since most financial companies hold some real assets, and most nonfinancial companies hold some financial assets. Rest assured that we use this working definition only as a support for our argument. We do not need it for our proposal to end banking.

How do nonfinancial companies apply the financial techniques? Most of these companies issue debt and equity. In other words, they *structure the liability side* of their balance sheet. Furthermore, their debt is usually of a shorter term than the time horizon of their business activities: nonfinancial companies *transform maturities*. Finally, they often pledge *collateral* to obtain better borrowing conditions. Even though nonfinancial companies apply a range of financial techniques, they do not create inside money. Recall the three features of inside money: It has to be perceived as risk-free and have the same denomination and liquidity as outside money. Debt of nonfinancial companies does not feature these characteristics.

First, debt of nonfinancial companies does not feature contractual liquidity.[16] Second, and more importantly, credit issued by nonfinancial companies carries significant credit risk. The profitability and, ultimately, the existence of nonfinancial companies rest upon a narrow range of goods or services. Idiosyncratic shocks on the markets they operate in have consequences on their ability to meet their financial obligations. Even large and reputable nonfinancial companies are unable to issue inside money.[17]

Why can financial companies create inside money while nonfinancial companies cannot? The answer lies in the composition of the asset side of balance sheets. In contrast to nonfinancial companies, financial ones hold credit contracts such as loans. A diversified portfolio of credit features less risk than a portfolio of real assets held by nonfinancial companies for two reasons.

First, holding credit contracts of a nonfinancial company on the asset side is already less risky than holding and operating the real assets of the same nonfinancial company. This results from the structure of the liability side of the nonfinancial company. Most risk from the asset side is borne by the shareholders of the nonfinancial company. Less risk remains with the credit contracts.

Second, financial companies can diversify their asset sides much better than nonfinancial companies. They usually hold credit from hundreds of different borrowers—for example, mortgages of individuals living in different places and loans of businesses operating in different markets. A financial company can therefore eliminate its vulnerability to idiosyncratic shocks to specific markets, whereas nonfinancial companies cannot.

Only financial companies can reduce credit risk to a degree that inside money creation becomes an option. Holding a diversified portfolio of credit on the asset side is, however, not yet sufficient to create inside money. Imagine a financial company that does so but refrains from structuring the liability side of its own balance sheet; that is, it only finances itself with equity. First, this company does not transform maturities—and as such, does not eliminate interest rate risk. Second, credit risk is still noticeable. Price fluctuations of financial assets are fully carried over to the company's equity. Inside money creation requires financial companies to take one more step: structure their liability sides, that is, issue a form of debt that features contractual liquidity.

Recall that traditional banking is the simplest possible application of financial techniques to create inside money. A bank holds a diversified portfolio of credit contracts on its asset side, and it structures its liability side into bank deposits and equity. Diversification reduces its vulnerability to idiosyncratic shocks. Structuring shields deposits from losses due to these idiosyncratic shocks. Pooling is done by granting loans with large notional amounts and by issuing deposits with smaller notional amounts. In addition, liquidity reserves on the asset side back the promise of contractual liquidity. While performed over several balance sheets, shadow banking applies the financial techniques in the same way as traditional banking.

Revisiting Double-Entry Bookkeeping

Thinking of banking as a particular application of financial techniques guides us toward an accounting rule that ends banking. For ease of understanding, we first formulate an updated technical solvency rule that prevents banking from being undertaken with all financial techniques except insurance. We have already introduced the concept of technical solvency in Part One. For a company to be technically solvent, the value of its assets must exceed the value of its liabilities; that is, the value of its equity must be positive. We propose updating the technical-solvency rule as follows:

> *The value of the real assets of a company has to be greater than or equal to the value of the company's liabilities.*

The only change to the current concept of technical solvency is that we have exchanged assets with real assets. What are real assets? *Real assets* are defined negatively as all assets that are not financial assets. A *financial asset* is an asset that appears on the liability side of another implicit or explicit balance sheet. The defining criterion for a financial asset is that it connects two distinct balance sheets. In the case of individuals and companies without financial reporting requirements, this is an implicit balance sheet.[18]

Credit contracts and equity claims are standard examples of financial assets.[19] Also, insurance and derivative contracts constitute financial assets for the beneficiary, as they appear as liabilities on the counterparty's balance sheet. Contrary to other definitions of financial assets, money does not fall under our definition. As we will see in the next chapter, money no longer connects two balance sheets in a financial system without banking. While holding money could be interpreted as holding a claim against society in general, it does not appear on the liability side of anybody's balance sheet.[20]

Hence, real assets include ownership claims on material and immaterial objects. Machinery and tools are examples of material objects. A patent is an example of an immaterial object. Physical existence is not a criterion for an asset to be real. If the asset is not financial, it is part of the real economy, and as such, it is a real asset. Only the balance sheet link determines whether an asset is deemed to be real or financial.

Let us define the second important concept of the updated solvency rule: *liabilities*. We already defined liabilities in Part One as obligations that a company has entered in the past, that is, everything a company owes. Let us be clear that any form of credit-equity hybrids such as preferred stocks or convertible bonds constitute a liability for the purpose of the updated solvency rule. Common equity is the only component of the liability side of a balance sheet that is not considered a liability. Defining equity so narrowly implies a broad definition of liabilities. Without a broad definition, companies could undermine the updated solvency rule with financial structures that involve different seniority levels of credit-equity hybrids.

The updated solvency rule applies to all companies. This is the only way to solve the boundary problem. While we differentiated between financial and nonfinancial companies for expositional purposes to derive the rule, the rule itself does not rely on such a distinction. It applies to all companies, but it does not apply to private persons. The reason is simple: Private persons are not able to create inside money in significant amounts. Private credit depends on the person backing it and always carries credit risk.[21]

Having described all the aspects of the updated solvency rule, let us illustrate its implications with an example. Assume that the equity of a company amounts to $40. Furthermore, this company takes up a loan of $60. If it allocates less than $40 in financial assets, it will meet the updated solvency rule. If it allocates more than $40 of its balance sheet in financial assets, it will violate the rule. Figure 9.1 depicts both situations.

Asset Side		Liability Side		Asset Side		Liability Side	
20	Financial assets	Liabilities	60	50	Financial assets	Liabilities	60
80	Real assets	(e.g., loans taken out)		50	Real assets	(e.g., loans taken out)	
		Equity	40			Equity	40
100	Total	Total	100	100	Total	Total	100

Figure 9.1 *The balance sheet of a company meeting (left side) and violating (right side) the updated solvency rule.*

Under the updated solvency rule, a company cannot fund financial assets with credit. In our example, the company can maximally hold $40 of financial assets, regardless of how much money the company borrows. It has to either hold all of its borrowed money in outside money for liquidity management or use it to acquire nonfinancial assets, such as real estate, structures, equipment, patents, or inventories.

We can read the updated solvency rule as: *The total value of financial assets of a company has to be less than or equal to the value of its equity.*

This reading highlights that companies have to back assets that are someone else's liability with their own funds, that is, equity. Companies cannot finance credit with someone else's credit.

While this might sound like a conservative investment advice, it prevents the formation of a daisy chain of balance sheets if applied on an economy-wide level. The solvency of one balance sheet no longer depends on the solvency of balance sheets further up the chain. As such, the updated solvency rule prevents companies from exposing their balance sheets to systemic financial risk.

Using deposits to finance loans, MBSs to finance mortgages, or repos to finance MBSs—all this is no longer possible under the updated solvency rule. The updated solvency rule effectively ends traditional banking and all current forms of shadow banking. Nonetheless, the updated solvency rule still allows the application of financial techniques to support a decentralized and capital-intensive economy in the digital age.

Disintermediated lending, such as peer-to-peer lending, is not restricted by the updated solvency rule. Peer-to-peer lending platforms do not hold financial assets on their balance sheet but only facilitate lending between third parties. The business model of mutual funds is also not affected by the updated solvency rule; any company can hold a diversified portfolio of financial assets if it is fully funded with equity.

One loophole for banking remains, however. The updated solvency rule allows for banking using insurance techniques. Imagine a financial company that only issues equity and holds a well-diversified portfolio of financial assets with low credit risk. This company—a mutual fund—has not created inside money. And under the updated solvency rule, it is not able do so by structuring its liability side. It could, however, obtain insurance from another financial company to turn its equity into inside money.

Such insurance would resemble the credit and liquidity guarantees we encountered when discussing ABCPs. The insurance could oblige the insuring company to always buy back the equity shares of the mutual fund at par if any current shareholder wishes to do so. If the promise is credible, then the shares of the mutual fund will become inside money; the insurance eliminates credit risk and offers contractual liquidity.

Knowing that a notification to the insuring company suffices to convert an equity share immediately at par into outside money, people will accept the equity shares as a medium of exchange. This implies that the insurance will actually be rarely invoked in normal times. As long as people believe in the credibility of the insurance contract, they do not have any reason to test it by converting the shares into outside money. In turn, the insuring company does not have to put aside many liquidity reserves to service its equity buy-back guarantee. We are back to banking.

The Systemic Solvency Rule

How can we prevent companies from abusing insurance techniques for banking? Carefully analyzing the links between balance sheets was sensible before, and it is again a good idea. The equity buy-back guarantee not only turns the mutual fund shares into inside money, it also appears as a liability on the balance sheet of the insuring company. The question is how the liability should be valued to determine whether a company is solvent. The valuation should be such that the insuring company is discouraged from participating in banking, but insurance techniques for sensible uses should still be possible. To achieve this, we propose the following systemic solvency rule:

> *The value of the real assets of a company has to be greater than or equal to the value of the company's liabilities in the worst financial state.*

The systemic solvency rule is a generalization of the updated solvency rule we discussed before. One additional concept—the worst financial state—has to be introduced to prevent insurance from being used for banking.

Before we can define the worst financial state, we need to introduce some additional definitions and concepts. Recall that a financial asset is defined as an asset that also appears on the liability side of another implicit or explicit balance sheet. Let a *financial contract* denote both the financial asset and the respective liability on the interlinked balance sheet. As such, the concept of the financial contract is closely related to that of a financial asset, but it is broader, as the liability related to a financial asset belongs to it, too.

We can further differentiate between contingent and noncontingent financial contracts. The nominal obligations of a *noncontingent financial contract* are fully determined upon writing it. A plain loan contract with fixed interest and fixed notional amount is such a contract. The counterparties of the contract agree at inception exactly how much money changes hands at what point in time; the nominal obligations are noncontingent on future events.

A financial contract for which the nominal obligation is not conclusively determined at inception is a *contingent financial contract*.[22] Derivatives and insurance contracts are prominent examples of contingent financial contracts. The nominal obligation of a fire insurance contract, for example, is not determined at inception. The contract constitutes a nominal obligation of zero for the insurance company once the contract expires and your house has not caught fire. In the event that your house burns down, you will calculate the damage, and the nominal obligation of the insurance company will be determined by the damage caused by the fire.

Contingent financial contracts determine the nominal obligation based on real events or financial events. A *financial event* is defined as the change in the state of another financial contract in terms of its valuation or contract specification at a certain point in time. For example, the market price of a particular stock at a particular point in time is a financial event. As such, an option to buy a particular stock at a particular time is a financial contract contingent on a financial event. Also, the occurrence of a borrower defaulting on a particular credit contract is a financial event. As such, a credit default swap is a financial contract contingent on a financial event. A change in the reference interest rate, which will be agreed upon for a particular credit contract at a particular time in the future, to determine the floating rate of an interest rate swap is a financial event as well.[23]

A *real event* is every event that is not a financial event. Your house catching fire is a real event. Furthermore, the market price of a real asset such as corn is also a real event, as it is determined by supply of and demand for a real asset. Note that a contingent financial contract that is contingent on a real event does not make it a real asset. It also falls under the definition of financial asset given above. Companies enjoying insurance or holding derivative contracts on the asset side have to treat these contracts as financial assets for calculating systemic solvency. Whether the contingency depends on a real event or on a financial event is, however, important for determining the worst financial state.

The *worst financial state* is given by the state in which all the financial events that are relevant for determining the nominal obligations arising from contingent financial contracts turn out in the most detrimental state for the value of a company's equity. The worst financial state does not depend on probabilities. It is conceptually different from risk weighting. The probability that a financial event can actually occur in reality does not matter for determining the worst financial state. The worst financial state is given by the legal characteristics of the contract and is not determined by statistical probabilities. If the legal obligation of a financial contract is unlimited, given the theoretically possible financial events, then the value of the contract in the worst financial state equals minus infinity.

The systemic solvency rule distinguishes between real risk sharing and financial risk shifting. This is why we call it the worst *financial* state. Today's accounting value of real insurance liabilities—sometimes called reserves—does not differ from the value in the worst financial state. An insurance company that insures real assets can record the resulting contingent financial contracts with the same value as today. The same is true for all contingent financial contracts that derive their value from real events. The valuations of liabilities arising from corn futures or oil forward contracts in the worst financial state, for example, do not differ from current accounting valuations. Such contingent contracts, however, have to be valued

Table 9.2 *The concept of the worst financial state exemplified*

Financial Contract	Worst Financial State	Value in the Worst Financial State
Loan	The borrower defaults, and the recovery value is zero.	$0
Equity	The company goes bankrupt, and nothing is left after serving the creditors of the company.	$0
Long CDS (i.e., buying credit protection, assuming upfront premium payment)	The credit protection is not tapped, or the counterparty of the CDS defaults.	$0
Short CDS (i.e., selling credit protection, receiving upfront premium payment)	The underlying security defaults, and the recovery value is zero.	minus the notional amount insured
Long a call option on one equity share	The share price ends below the strike price of the call option, or the counterparty defaults.	$0
Short a call option on one equity share	Theoretically, there is no upper limit on the price of an equity share.	minus infinity
Short a call option on one equity share and owning one equity share	The equity share price drops to zero. In this case, the value is zero, and the call option will not be exercised.	$0
Long a put option on one equity share	The share price ends above the strike price of the put option, or the counterparty defaults.	$0
Short a put option on one equity share	The equity share price drops to zero, and the put option is exercised by the buyer.	minus the strike price
Repo	The repo borrower defaults, and the value of the financial asset used as collateral falls to zero.	$0

at zero for calculating systemic solvency, if they appear on the asset side of a company's balance sheets.

In contrast to the valuation of contingent financial contracts that derive their value from real events, the ones that derive their value from financial events will be valued differently in the worst financial state. For example, market prices of equity claims can end up anywhere between $0 and infinity. Hence, the seller of an equity call option—a contingent financial contract that derives its value from a financial event—has a theoretically unlimited loss potential.[24] To provide another example, the reference rate for an interest rate swap could end up anywhere; the parties involved in setting the reference rate could agree on any interest rate. Hence, an interest rate swap becomes an infinite value liability in the worst financial state. A credit guarantee is an example of a financial contract for which the worst financial state results in a bounded value. If a company provides a credit guarantee for a loan, the value of the credit guarantee in the worst financial state is minus the notional amount of the loan. In Table 9.2, we have listed the worst financial states for some financial contracts to clarify the concept.

An important remark is in order. Certain contingent financial contracts can switch from the asset side to the liability side or vice versa over their lifetime. An interest rate swap, for example, is a contingent financial contract for which one party—the so-called receiver—receives a fixed interest rate and pays a floating interest rate that is linked to a reference rate. If the expected reference rate of the interest rate swap is lower than the fixed interest rate, the current valuation is positive and the interest rate swap appears as an asset on the balance sheet of the receiver.[25] As soon as the reference rate exceeds the fixed interest rate, the interest rate swap switches from the asset side to the liability side of the receiver's balance sheet.

Hence, a financial contract that is currently accounted for as a financial asset can turn to a liability in the worst financial state. In the case of the interest rate swap, for instance, the worst financial state is given by the reference interest rate increasing to infinity. In this case, the interest rate swap becomes a liability. For the valuation of a financial contract in the worst financial state, it does not matter whether it is currently accounted for on the asset side or on the liability side. For the purposes of calculating systemic solvency under the new rule, a contingent financial contract that currently appears as a financial asset can become a liability.

The systemic solvency rule closes the last loophole and makes it impractical to use insurance techniques for the purpose of banking. Let us clarify this thought along the example used before. Recall that the mutual fund raised $100 of equity and invested it in a diversified portfolio of financial assets. This mutual fund searches for an insurance company that sells an equity buy-back guarantee to turn its equity into inside money.

Imagine that an insurance company considers issuing such a guarantee for the mutual fund. The equity buy-back guarantee would constitute a contingent financial contract. The nominal value of the obligation depends on the future value of the mutual fund's equity—it depends on a financial event. As such, the insurance company needs to calculate the worst possible financial state for the guarantee and check that its liability will not become larger than the value of its real assets.

The worst financial state of the equity buy-back guarantee is unambiguous. It is the state in which the equity share of the mutual fund becomes completely worthless, and all shareholders sell their shares to the insurance company. Hence, the liability of the equity buy-back guarantee is $100 in the worst possible financial state. Assuming that it has no other liabilities, the insurance company needs to hold at least $100 of either outside money or real assets before offering the guarantee. Both asset types are particularly ill-suited for backing inside money creation. Holding the $100 in real assets is not viable because of storage costs. It is less costly to just hold outside money than real assets, but backing inside money creation with outside money undermines its purpose. $100 of outside money is required to create $100 of inside money. Under the systemic solvency rule, providing financial insurance for the purpose of banking turns out to be economically infeasible.

Why the Systemic Solvency Rule Should be Implemented to End Banking

Both narrow banking and limited purpose banking fall prey to the boundary problem, just as traditional banking regulation does. They try to get a grip on the problems with banking at an institutional level and regulate companies that are called banks or financial institutions. Banking, however, is a creature of double-entry bookkeeping. In the digital age, banking will always find its way through unregulated companies.

The systemic solvency rule addresses the problem where it originates, at the level of accounting. Our approach does not rely on a legally difficult distinction between banks and nonbanks or between financial and nonfinancial institutions. The virtue of the systemic solvency rule lies in its universality. It applies to the balance sheet of every company.

Nevertheless, nonfinancial companies will hardly feel any impact by the new solvency rule. On the liability side of the balance sheets of nonfinancial companies, equity usually accounts for 30% to 40% of total liabilities.[26] On the asset side of their balance sheet, nonfinancial companies hold mostly real assets. The value of real assets of nonfinancial companies in the United States is on average greater than the value of their liabilities.[27] Most nonfinancial companies already comply with the new solvency rule. Some companies will need to deleverage, that is, raise more equity or sell some financial assets. Nevertheless, no business model in the nonfinancial sector is endangered by the systemic solvency rule.[28]

The systemic solvency rule effectively targets banking. As such, financial companies that do not perform banking have more freedom than if they were subject to a narrow banking or limited purpose banking regime. This can be seen by the fact that the systemic solvency rule contains both proposals. Narrow banks that hold 100% of their liabilities as money comply with the new rule. So do limited purpose banks that are fully funded with equity.

It appears paradoxical, but the fact that the systemic solvency rule is all-encompassing makes it less restrictive than the institutional approaches to regulate banking. Since institutional approaches—such as traditional capital requirements, narrow banking, or limited purpose banking—always struggle with the boundary problem, regulators have to continuously adapt and expand their regulations. Regulators become increasingly interventionist over time, as they try to keep their grip on banking. Institutional banking regulation tends to become more complex and more constraining over time.

In contrast, the systemic solvency rule allows for total flexibility within the clear-cut boundaries it sets. The new rule allows for a variety of financial business models that have no place in narrow banking or limited purpose banking. The systemic solvency rule ends banking but leaves everything what is happening inside its boundaries to dynamic competition. No unnecessary restrictions are imposed, for instance, on financial institutions that operate in disintermediated lending channels; neither peer-to-peer lenders nor financial advisors are affected by it.

In addition, the systemic solvency rule is simple to enforce without creating the bureaucratic overkill we have become so accustomed to with current banking regulation. The restrictions imposed by the new rule can be monitored by certified public accountants and external auditors who are already verifying balance sheets today. Private persons and partnerships with full liability are not subject to the new solvency rule and do not have to be monitored. Introducing the systemic solvency rule allows for canceling a lot of existing costly regulation and dissolve enforcement agencies while not requiring any new institutions.

Ending banking is a delicate task. Institutional approaches are doomed to fail because of the boundary problem. Only tackling the task at the fundamental level of accounting will succeed. The origin of banking lies in double-entry bookkeeping, and so does the end of banking.

—————————————— NOTES ——————————————

1. Haldane (2012b, 15)

2. Governments cannot commit not to insure banking risks. We have seen this repeatedly in history, most recently with the bailout of shadow banking institutions during the financial crisis of 2007–08 (see Part Two). Bank bailout policies suffer from the problem of time inconsistency. For analytical models of the time-inconsistency problem in banking, see Mailath and Mester (1994), Acharya and Yorulmazer (2007), Farhi and Tirole (2012), and Chari and Kehoe (2013).

3. One can escape banking risk to a certain degree by holding real claims, such as ownership claims on real estate, equity claims, or precious metals. Almost everyone needs, however, money for transactional purposes and is therefore still exposed to banking risk. Furthermore, you cannot avoid banking risk if bailouts are financed by taxes.

4. For example, some peer-to-peer lending platforms are already moving toward banking. They have started to provide credit insurance in case borrowers default. One example is given by Zopa's "Safeguard fund," see https://www.zopa.com/lending/peer-to-peer-experts. Such an insurance scheme transforms peer-to-peer credit contracts almost into inside money.

5. A well-known and influential proponent of narrow banking is Fisher (1935). Furthermore, Friedman (1965) and Tobin (1985, 1987) indicated their support for narrow banking.

6. See Fisher (1935).

7. Diamond and Rajan (2001) stress the importance of banks transforming illiquid assets into liquid deposits and use it as an argument against stabilization policies such as narrow banking. See also Wallace (1996) and Bossone (2001).

8. As a matter of fact, Fisher and his colleagues have been aware that their proposal runs into the boundary problem. One of the letters of Simons—a supporter of the 100% money proposal—to Fisher says "savings-deposits, treasury certificates, and even commercial paper are almost as close to demand deposits as are demand deposits to legal-tender currency. The whole problem which we now associate with commercial banking might easily reappear in other forms of financial arrangements" (Allen, 1993, p. 708). Simons had foreseen the rise of shadow banking as early as 1934 (see also Simons 1936).

9. Benes and Kumhof (2012) analyze the effects of narrow banking using a dynamic stochastic general equilibrium model. Unfortunately, their model does not account for the boundary problem.

10. The positive money movement was founded in 2010 as a reaction to the financial crisis. For an introduction to the positive money proposal, see Jackson, Dyson, and Hodgson (2013).

11. Huber and Robertson (2000, chap. 4), the early mentors of positive money, call this privilege the "special banking profits." While we identify a different underlying mechanism, the profits earned by financial sector companies during the 20 years leading up to the crisis were indeed stellar. According to the U.S. Bureau of Economic Analysis (2013, 2014), around 10% of all corporate profits were earned in the financial sector in 1950. In the years prior to the financial crisis of 2007–08, this share increased to above 25%. Furthermore, not everything a company earns is paid out as profit. A large share goes to its employees. In 2006, employees earned on average 50% more in finance (Philippon and Reshef 2012). For executives, the premium is even higher.

12. See Kotlikoff (2010). For a later succinct account, see Chamley, Kotlikoff, and Polemarchakis (2012).

13. O'Driscoll (2010, 545), highlights this by citing Kotlikoff (2010): "The FFA would verify Robby's income statement using federal income tax returns; it would certify his credit rating; it would verify, using independent local appraisers, the value of the home he intends to purchase; it would verify the property taxes and insurance costs on the home; and it would specify all other pertinent information that would help a mutual fund understand the value of buying Robby's mortgage" (p. 127).

14. As a case in point, Sapienza (2002) compared the lending behavior of state-owned versus private banks in Italy. She concluded that state-owned banks base their lending decisions on political considerations. State-owned banks charged less interest in regions in which the political party affiliated with the bank was stronger. As with state-owned banks, the power over lending decisions by the FFA could equally tempt governments to use it as a device for rewarding political supporters and punishing political opponents.

15. See Chapter 4.

16. Most credit issued by nonfinancial companies has a maturity of years. Nonfinancial companies operate with a long time horizon and cannot risk rolling over too much of their credit every single day. The loans with the shortest time of maturities issued by nonfinancial companies are commercial papers (CPs) with a maturity of a few days. Compared to other credit sources such as bank loans or corporate bonds, the volume of CPs is marginal.

17. As of April 2014, Standard & Poor's granted only three nonfinancial companies in the United States an AAA rating: Exxon Mobil, Johnson & Johnson, and Microsoft (Krantz 2014). Credit issued by nonfinancial companies usually carries quite some credit risk.

18. An implicit balance sheet is, for example, the balance sheet of an individual person. If you have a mortgage and own a house, you would put the value of your house on the asset side and the mortgage on the liability side. As such, the mortgage is a financial asset even though it does not appear on an explicit balance sheet.

19. Equity claims include strategic holdings of subsidiaries by a parent company.

20. In the current banking system with a central bank, outside money appears as a liability on the central bank's balance sheet. In a financial system without banking, monetary policy is conducted differently (see Chapter 10).

21. A personal event of a private borrower, such as an accident, can drastically change the credit risk. The same reasoning applies to private partnerships or sole proprietorships. There are some isolated cases of banks that operate as private partnerships, mainly offering their services for wealthy clients. The owners of these banks are fully responsible for any of the banks' liability with their personal wealth. Investment banks used to be organized as private partnerships, but nowadays banks organized as private partnerships are rare.

22. Some financial contracts have both contingent and noncontingent components. A floating rate loan, for instance, has a predetermined repayment of the notional amount, but the interest payments are contingent on how a future reference rate is determined. For our purposes, we should treat such contracts as two. The notional repayment, which is fixed, constitutes a noncontingent financial contract, while the variable interest payments constitute a contingent financial contract.

23. Reference interest rates are used to determine the floating interest-rate payments of loans or of interest rate swaps. A well-known reference rate is the London Interbank Offered Rate (LIBOR).

24. An equity *call option* is the right to buy an equity share at a particular price and at a particular point in time or over a particular period of time.

25. In accounting, such a position is called a *positive replacement value*. It is the profit that accrued as the expectations of future contingent events changed. For example, if the reference rate of an interest rate swap was expected to be 5%, but increases to 7% over time, the interest rate swap will appear as an asset on the balance sheet of the counterparty who receives floating rates and pays fix rates. Conversely, if it falls to 3%, then the interest rate swap will appear as a negative replacement value on the liability side. Such swaps are usually agreed at a fixed rate that the present value of all expected floating rate payments equals the present value of all fixed rate payments, that is, at a replacement value of 0.

26. See Rajan and Zingales (1995) who conducted an international study on the capital structure of public nonfinancial corporations. Compared to banks, nonfinancial companies hold considerably more equity because they do not enjoy government guarantees. They have to hold high levels of equity to demonstrate to their lenders that they have enough skin in the game.

27. See Rajan and Zingales (1995, 1428). In Table II, they show the average balance sheets for nonfinancial corporations in the G7 countries in 1991. The numbers indicate that the value of financial assets including cash is lower than shareholders' equity in the United States, Canada, and the United Kingdom.

28. Depending on the industry companies operate in, capital structures can differ. Electronic and pharmaceutical companies, for instance, rely little on external finance (Mayer 1990). For a recent study on legal and industry-specific factors, see, for example, de Jong, Kabir, and Nguyen (2008). In particular, some companies operate with large accounts receivable. *Accounts receivable* arise if a company has already delivered goods and services to the customer, but has not received full payment yet. Such billing practices can lead to conflicts with the systemic solvency rule. A gradual change in these practices can realign the capital structure of companies running large accounts receivable. Reasons usually put forward in economic theory to motivate a certain capital structure do not consider accounts receivable (see, e.g., Dewatripont and Tirole 1994).

<u>10</u> The Role of the Public Sector

Ending banking involves redefining the role of the public sector in the organization of the financial system. A financial system without banking would no longer feature banking panics. Governments would no longer have to guarantee the liabilities of any private institution to safeguard the financial system. In a financial system without banking, the rationale for banking regulation would fall away, and the government would assume a new role in the organization of credit.

Since banking is the creation of money out of credit, ending banking also impacts the organization of money. The distinction between inside and outside money ceases to be of any use. Monetary policy needs to be reconsidered because it is currently built around banks and the creation of inside money. As with credit, we have to redefine the role of public institutions in the organization of money.

Public Organization of Money

Recall the function of money in the financial system: Money is used for current payment. It is essential for a decentralized economy. The use of money as a medium of exchange leads to the formation of prices that coordinate economic activities.

Prices should reflect economic conditions without distortions originating from the financial system. In the introduction, we interpreted money and credit as the mirror, while prices were the picture of the real economy within this mirror. Distortions in the price system lead to a blurred picture of economic conditions and in turn to misallocations.

The objective of the organization of money is clear: Money should be organized such that systematic price distortions are avoided. Changes in the amount of money in circulation should not lead to an unexpected fall or rise in the price level. Prices should not be distorted by the organization of money. In other words, we should aim for a functioning price system—that is, price stability—when organizing money.[1]

A functioning price system is a classic public good, as undistorted prices are neither rivalrous nor excludable. Besides its public-good character, a functioning price system is also a network good. As such, the provision of a price system can be considered a natural monopoly. One functioning price system is more efficient than many price systems. Both network effects and the public-good nature of a functioning price system suggest that organizing money is a public affair.[2]

Monetary policy is already in public hands today. Yet, it has to be adapted to a financial system without banking. The currently used tools of monetary policy are no longer an option. In a financial system without banking, central *banking* makes no sense. There is no reason for a central bank to act as a lender of last resort and to offer privileged access to money to a selected group of private institutions. Both the tools of monetary policy and the institutional setup of the monetary authority need to be reconsidered.

Digital Money for Price Stability in the Digital Age

Before we discuss the tools of monetary policy, let us emphasize once more its goal: price stability. We should aim for a functioning price system when devising new tools for monetary policy. Moving from paper-based to digital money supports this goal. A financial system in the digital age leaves no room for physical money.

At first sight, this might seem like a radical change. But note that a large quantity of outside money—the central bank reserves of banks—already exists in digital form only. In addition, almost all of our daily payments in inside money are conducted electronically. Be it the payment of a coffee by card or of a book online, in neither of these cases is physical cash exchanged.

Electronic money raises privacy concerns that need to be addressed. The public sector is well advised to address people's desire to conduct anonymous economic exchanges. If it does not, it is likely that some private institutions will step in and satisfy the demand by offering anonymous payment services.

There are several advantages to digital money.[3] Most important for the organization of the financial system, digital money allows for monetary tools that are powerful in providing price stability. In particular, we can deal much more effectively with the zero lower bound, as a liquidity fee can be implemented without any administrative burden.

Addressing the Zero Lower Bound with a Liquidity Fee

A liquidity fee is a fee raised from money holders, similar to a toll raised from drivers on a toll road. It can be compared to a negative interest rate on money holdings. For example, if you keep $100 of money for one year in your (digital) pocket, and the annual liquidity fee amounts to 5%, you will end up with $95 at the end of one year. The liquidity fee is raised continuously, and its effects are comparable to inflation. If you hold $100 in cash and inflation amounts to 5%, you will lose approximately $5 in purchasing power, the same you would pay with a 5% liquidity fee and zero inflation.[4]

Today, central banks aim at a positive inflation rate to deal with the zero lower bound.[5] A positive inflation rate relaxes the restriction imposed by the zero lower bound that nominal interest rates cannot fall below zero. With inflation, people continuously lose purchasing power on money holdings. They are incentivized to spend money or lend it to someone else even if interest rates are low. The economic effects of inflation are similar to those of a liquidity fee.

Inflation features, however, uncertainty and high costs. Inflation is not an ideal tool to deal with the zero lower bound. Inflation is hard to control because it depends just as much on people's expectations as on actual monetary policy. We have seen that it is difficult to provoke inflation if the economy is already at the zero lower bound.[6] Once inflation picks up, it can easily get out of hand, severely distorting the price system. Besides that, unexpected inflation creates costs because people have to adapt to changes in the overall price level.[7]

A liquidity fee removes the zero lower bound without featuring the uncertainty and costs that are inherent to inflation. Historically, the liquidity fee was impractical because of the administrative burden it would have created. Imagine collecting a monthly fee on every banknote and coin that exists within the economy. This drawback falls away with digital money. In this case, the liquidity fee can be applied continuously at negligible costs.[8]

A liquidity fee removes money from circulation by its very design. To provide for price stability, the monetary authority also needs a tool to inject money into circulation. A simple and effective tool to inject money is an unconditional income.

Injecting Money with an Unconditional Income

Proposing an unconditional income as a tool for monetary policy is unusual. But it is the perfect tool for monetary policy to pursue price stability. Considering unconditional income as a monetary policy tool also exposes the unfair setup of monetary policy in our current banking system. We cannot think of any reason a few private institutions should have a privileged access to money. In our current banking system *some animals are more equal than others*.

An unconditional income, on the contrary, is equal by design. The independent monetary authority issues new money by simply transferring it to the citizens. Everyone receives the same amount of unconditional income regardless of any personal characteristics, for example, employment status or age. Hence, the concept is close to a basic income guarantee.[9]

Unconditional income used as a monetary policy instrument, however, is too low to enable a standard of living above the poverty line. It would be misleading to call it *basic* income. Furthermore, unconditional income is only a means to an end—the end being price stability. As such, it cannot remain fixed and is thus not a *guaranteed* income. The public monetary authority will have to occasionally adjust the amount of unconditional income to maintain price stability in a dynamic economic environment.

Today, the profits of outside money creation by central banks are usually channeled to governments.[10] Some narrow banking proposals, such as positive money, want to keep this arrangement by handing over newly issued money directly to governments. We oppose this view. Our preference for unconditional income might seem to be of minor relevance if the government represents the people. But injecting money via an unconditional income has two important advantages.

First and most important, distributing unconditional income continuously among the population puts monetary policy immediately and broadly into effect. People use their unconditional income either to consume or to invest. If money was, however, injected via government expenses, political processes would affect how, where, and when money entered the economy. The effects on the price system would become less immediate and discontinuous. To achieve price stability, government spending is an inferior monetary policy tool. The same can be said about current monetary policy, which also distorts prices. Today's central banks inject money by buying financial assets what affects the prices of these assets. Only the monetary policy tool of unconditional income allows money to be injected without distorting prices.[11]

Second, political pressure on the monetary authority is higher in a system where money is injected via the government. Such a setup might tempt governments to increase seignorage at the expense of price stability. If the monetary authority is bound by the constitution to only inject new money via an unconditional income, government interference on monetary policy is mitigated.

Independence of Monetary Policy

Let us reemphasize that unconditional income is a by-product of monetary policy, not an objective. The only objective is price stability. A strict rule-based framework should govern the use of monetary policy tools for the sole purpose of fostering price stability.

In contrast to the monetary policy instruments used today, both the liquidity fee and the unconditional income are fully transparent, easy to understand, and egalitarian by design. If the monetary authority intended to use its tools in a way not to pursue price stability, it could only subsidize everybody by increasing the unconditional income or taxing everybody by increasing the liquidity fee. Without openly breaking constitutional rules, it is hard to provide particular interest groups with an advantage or to bail out private institutions using monetary policy. To further shield monetary policy from political influence, it should be set up as independently as possible from the other branches of government.[12]

The Relationship of Monetary Policy to Fiscal Policy

A strict rule-based setting with independence from the government breaks the intimate link between monetary and fiscal policy. Today, the central bank not only channels its profits to the government, it also uses government bonds to conduct monetary policy. We have discussed how the Fed's holdings of government debt rose to unprecedented levels after the financial crisis of 2007–08. Furthermore, recall that capital requirements encourage banks to hold government debt. If the government struggles to serve its debt, central banks are forced to step in, because otherwise banks will quickly suffer losses that eventually escalate in banking panics and distortions of the price system.

In a financial system without banking, the monetary authority can credibly commit not to bail out governments. In turn, governments are forced to run a sustainable—though not necessarily balanced—budget. Without overthrowing the constitutional rule that monetary policy is bound to the two instruments of the liquidity fee and unconditional income, the monetary authority can neither buy nor guarantee government debt. Governments can no longer stealthily spread the costs of unsustainable expenses on everybody by provoking inflation.

If the government cannot serve its debt, it will have no choice but to default and negotiate with its creditors. When the government defaults, everyone holding government debt will suffer losses.

Because of the systemic solvency rule, however, second-round effects are absent and no systemic crisis is triggered. Anyone who is not exposed to government debt will not suffer losses. If governments can default without risking the functionality of the financial system, people will become more cautious in lending money to the government. They will carefully monitor the sustainability of the government budget. If they think that the government is not acting responsibly, they can ask for higher interest rates or refuse to lend money altogether. To spend more money than it earns, the government will have to gain the trust from potential lenders, that is, from its citizens.[13]

Private Organization of Credit

The systemic solvency rule prevents systemic effects emanating not only from government defaults but also from defaults in general. Credit organized under the systemic solvency rule has no network characteristics. It is also not a public good. The justifications we found for organizing money as a public affair are not prevalent in the realm of credit.

In a financial system without banking, governments should give up any guarantees of credit that have their roots in preventing banking panics. In particular, deposit insurance, lender-of-last-resort facilities, or all-encompassing too-big-to-fail guarantees are superfluous under the systemic solvency rule.

Without government guarantees, the reason for extensive regulation vanishes, too. Governments no longer need to deal with risk-weighted capital requirements, internal risk-management models, reserve requirements, and countless other forms of regulations that shape the current organization of credit.

Credit no longer requires a special treatment in a financial system without banking. Government should implement a competitive regulatory framework around credit that treats the financial industry just like any other industry. In essence, such a framework includes an effective and efficient legal system to enforce private contracts, the prosecution of market participants that engage in fraudulent practices, and antitrust laws to ensure that markets are not cartelized or monopolized by powerful actors.[14]

Contrary to money, credit belongs to the private sphere. Credit will flourish within a competitive regulatory framework. Just as companies develop better and cheaper products in other industries, a competitive credit market will become better at providing liquidity, managing credit risk, and addressing information asymmetries.

---------------------- NOTES ----------------------

1. Most contemporary central banks have a mandate to maintain price stability. They define a bundle of goods and services and monitor the price of the bundle. Central banks usually target the price of this bundle to grow in a certain range, generally around 2%; that is, they commit to price-growth stability. One reason for not targeting price-level stability—that is, a zero inflation rate—lies in nominal price rigidities. Price rigidities occur when prices cannot adjust, although a new price is required to clear supply and demand. One prominent example is given by price rigidities on labor markets. It is considered to be particularly hard to adjust wages downward; see, for example, Akerlof et al. (1996).

2. See Simons (1936), who considers securing a monetary system as an important objective of the public. Such a system should feature as little monetary uncertainty as possible. See also M. Friedman (1948, 1965), who justified a government monopoly for outside money based on similar reasons. Note, however, that he qualified his opinion in a later paper in light of the experience with high inflation during the 1970s and early 1980s (M. Friedman and Schwartz 1986). On the network effects, see also King (2004). Notwithstanding our preference for a public organization of money, we would refrain from prohibiting privately issued currencies. Privately issued currencies can complement the payment system. Furthermore, prohibiting private currencies would inevitably run into the boundary problem as many nonfinancial businesses issue vouchers and coupons for their goods and services.

3. Digital money is considered to be more convenient than physical money. As a consumer, you do not need to carry cash around with you, and so the risk of theft is lower (see, e.g., Wright et al. 2014). For businesses, the advantages are even more pronounced, as they would no longer need to manage physical cashiers and ship physical money to and from their stores. Humphrey et al. (2003) provide an estimate of the gains from shifting from physical to digital money. Finally, health reasons are mentioned as a further advantage of digital money, as some studies indicate that bank notes are bacterially contaminated (see, e.g., Pope et al. 2002).

4. A liquidity fee has been recently proposed by various economists; see Goodfriend (2000), Buiter and Panigirtzoglou (2003), and Mankiw (2009). The earliest proponent

of a liquidity fee was Gesell (1916), whose intentions were broader than just overcoming the zero lower bound. Be aware that notation varies. Some use the term *dying money*, following Gesell (e.g., Preparata and Elliott 2004), or *stamp scrip* (Fisher 1933b). Today, the term *carry tax* is often used; see Goodfriend (2000) and Buiter and Panigirtzoglou (2003). We chose the term *liquidity fee* because the term *carry tax* would be misleading. It is not a tool to generate revenue for the public sector. As we will see, the money raised with the liquidity fee reenters the economy with an unconditional income, and the public sector cannot use it to finance its own activities.

5. See Chapter 7. For a discussion of the rationale to pursue a positive inflation rate, see, for example, Summers (1991) or Fischer (1996).

6. See also Goodfriend (2000).

7. Direct consequences of frequent price changes are, for example, so-called menu costs, that is, the costs of redesigning price lists. More important are, however, indirect costs of inflation, such as inefficiencies in the coordination of economic activities. See also Lucas (2000).

8. The advantages of the liquidity fee have been recognized by other economists as well. See Goodfriend (2000), Buiter and Panigirtzoglou (2003), and Mankiw (2009). One way proposed to implement a liquidity fee in the industrial age was to stamp banknotes monthly against a fee (see Fisher 1933b). Mankiw (2009) proposed that the monetary authority could periodically pick a random number out of a hat. All banknotes whose serial numbers end with that number would cease to be legal tender. Both proposals illustrate that before the rise of information technology, a liquidity fee would have been indeed impractical.

9. A basic income guarantee aims at enabling every citizen to live a life of dignity. Often, basic income guarantees are supposed to replace existing social insurances. Proponents highlight its nondistortionary effect, as it basically reflects a lump sum subsidy to every individual.

10. Some profits arising within the Federal Reserve System are also paid to private banking institutions due to a special institutional setup: Member banks receive a statutory dividend.

11. In a financial system without banking, monetary policy cannot affect particular prices by its very design. New money is not injected by buying assets but by being distributed equally among the population. Note also that money is created outside the accounting system, that is, off balance sheets. This is the reason money does not qualify as a financial asset for the systemic solvency rule. In today's banking system, issuing money is reflected on central banks' balance sheets: the assets bought are reported on the asset side and the new money is reported on the liability side.

12. Recall that when we discussed limited purpose banking, we criticized the setup of a single authority for the supervision of monitoring. But now we call for an independent monetary authority with full control over the money supply. At first

sight, it might seem that we are not applying the same standards to our concepts. But the management of the money supply and the supervision of the monitoring of all credit in the economy are two different things. A monetary authority that is bound by the constitution to only use a liquidity fee and an unconditional income finds it hard to abuse its power. Both tools are ill-suited to pursue the particular interests of people at the monetary authority given that they always target—by their very design—everyone. A governmental monitoring agency, on the other hand, decides who gets credit when and at what conditions. For people in charge, such a setup is attractive to pursue their particular interests.

13. While governments are no companies, the systemic solvency rule should conceptually also apply to them. Credit should only be used to invest in real assets for which governments expect to generate enough (tax) returns to meet future obligations.

14. Today, the opposite is actually the case. While banks have to implement countless specific regulation, too-big-to-fail banks seem to be exempt from some common legal obligations. In connection with prosecuting HSBC for money-laundering offenses, U.S. Attorney General Eric Holder admitted that the fact that these banks are so large "has an inhibiting influence—impact on our ability to bring resolutions that I think would be more appropriate." (Nasiripour and Scanell 2013).

<u>11</u> The Big Picture

Over the course of this book, we have introduced numerous economic concepts, accounting fundamentals, and institutions. We have come a long way, and it is now time to look at the big picture. Switching to a macroeconomic perspective unveils the essence of our reform proposals. A financial system without banking is different from a banking system in two fundamental ways: It separates the functions of money and credit, and it sets clear boundaries between the public and the private spheres.

Unconstrained Banking Leads to Misallocations

We noted in the introduction that the financial system is the virtual counterpart to the real economy. Only with a functional financial system can undistorted prices form. The organization of money and credit influences how well prices fulfill their economic function. Recall that prices coordinate all economic activities, including the accumulation of capital.

Banking affects the organization of both money and credit. The advantage of banking is that it enhanced capital accumulation in the industrial age. It did so at the cost of severely distorting the price system during banking panics. The simultaneous, rapid destruction of money and credit inhibited real economic activity and amplified recessions.

Before the digital revolution, it was possible to get a grip on the problems with banking by combining government guarantees and banking regulations. Government guarantees prevented banking panics and sudden collapses in money and credit. At the same time, banking regulations prevented excessive risk taking that would have resulted in the opposite: an unconstrained and rapid expansion of money and credit.

In Part Two, we discussed extensively how the digital revolution has impaired the functionality of a banking system. Information technology opened up ways to circumvent banking regulation. The constraints intended to curb excessive risk taking have become ineffective. Banks could not resist the opportunity and created huge amounts of inside money off their own balance sheets. The result was a shadow banking boom in the run up to the financial crisis of 2007–08.

The banking-fueled economic boom distorted prices and led to misallocations in the real economy. The excessive amounts of money and credit created by unconstrained banking drove up both the demand and the prices for real estate. Distorted price signals triggered a construction frenzy. Labor, physical capital, and energy were used to build housing units for which there was eventually no real demand.[1]

The distortions of unconstrained banking are enticing during a boom phase. They create the illusion of economic growth and wealth creation. Investment activities are expanded, employment picks up, consumption increases, and asset prices rise. People warning of an impending crash are vilified as alarmists and ignored. But the ensuing crisis forcefully proves them right. In the end, all that unconstrained banking does is create an unsustainable credit bubble that eventually bursts.[2]

Once the bubble bursts, people realize that resources were wasted. Prices adjust forcefully, which threatens the solvency of many borrowers. The resulting defaults quickly escalate into a banking panic in a sector that is not safeguarded by government guarantees. The original problem with banking, which was considered to be solved, reappears in a new place.

As in classic banking panics, the sudden collapse of money and credit distorts the price system. This time, the effects on prices do not trigger a boom but a severe recession. The economy enters a downward spiral of credit destruction, monetary contraction, and falling prices. Investment stalls, unemployment rises and consumption decreases.[3]

Through boom and bust, unconstrained banking leads to welfare losses. The overshooting creation and destruction of money and credit in an unconstrained banking system distorts prices, leading to misallocations of resources in the real economy. The source of the distortion is the tight link banking creates between money and credit, and the digital revolution is the reason the regulatory framework can no longer contain price distortions.

Assigning the Proper Functions to Money and Credit

Unconstrained banking distorts the price system because money and credit are two sides of the same coin in a banking system. The functions of money and credit as media for current and deferred payment, are not assigned properly. Credit—in the form of inside money—can be used for current payment. In addition, money can become a suitable medium for deferred payment at the zero lower bound. Figure 11.1 illustrates today's banking system.

The new solvency rule breaks the intimate link banking creates between money and credit. It assigns the current payment function exclusively to money. The monetary authority can exert full control over the quantity of money in circulation, because credit can no longer be transformed into money. Under a systemic solvency rule, credit extension does not lead to money creation.

Extending credit is only possible if those owning money are willing to give up their purchasing power today in exchange for purchasing power in the future. In a financial system without banking, the interest rate becomes a meaningful price for exchanging purchasing power. Credit expansion shifts current purchasing power from lenders to borrowers. Correspondingly, credit contraction merely shifts purchasing power from borrowers back to lenders. It

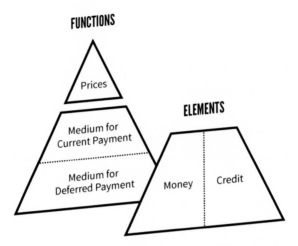

Figure 11.1 A financial system with banking: part one

does not decrease the quantity of money, and it does not lead to a downward pressure on prices for real goods and services. Without banking, the quantity of money no longer directly depends on the quantity of outstanding credit.

An indirect effect, however, exists between money and credit, given that the monetary authority pursues price stability. Credit used for productive investments increases the capacity of the economy to produce real goods and services. In this case, the same quantity of money meets a larger quantity of real goods and services on the market. Prices fall. Falling prices induce the monetary authority to act on its price stability mandate and to increase the quantity of money.

As such, credit that is used productively will eventually increase the quantity of money. Credit used for unproductive purposes, however, will not do so. In a financial system without banking, money will "wait" and see what businesses and individuals do with credit. If credit is used productively, the quantity of money will grow.

The quantity of money is not the sole determinant of the money supply, that is, the effective supply of a medium for current payment. The money supply also depends on whether people spend or hoard their money. In other words, the velocity of circulation matters as well. An additional dollar that is never spent increases the quantity of money, but not the money supply. This brings us to the second link between money and credit, which is not related to banking but to the physical nature of today's money.

Money can be used as a store of value. Money used as a store of value is no longer a device for current payment. To see this, we have to adopt the perspective of the money holder, who is a potential lender. If the money holder keeps money to pay for goods and services tomorrow, money functions as a medium for deferred payment. As such, hoarded money is used in a similar way as credit. If people hoard money, the demand for real goods and services declines, and prices deflate. This is what happened after the financial crisis of 2007–08, with central bank reserves sitting idle on bank's balance sheets after the federal funds rate hit the zero lower bound.

Deflation increases the real return on holding money and makes money more attractive as a store of value. Interest rates at the zero lower bound can lead to a collapse of the velocity of circulation and trap the economy in a deflationary spiral. Again, the link between money and credit—this time originating from the store of value function of physical money—is the cause for a distortion of prices.

The liquidity fee cuts the second link between money and credit, because it discourages people from using money for deferred payment—that is, from hoarding money. The liquidity fee completes the functional separation of money into a device for current payment, and credit into a device for deferred payment. Figure 11.2 visualizes how we envision a financial system in the digital age.

Money and credit are the means to establish the price system that is required to coordinate the activities in the real economy. For prices to be undistorted, the function of current payment needs to be assigned to money, and that of deferred payment to credit. A functional separation alone, however, is not sufficient; we also need to separate the public from the private sphere.

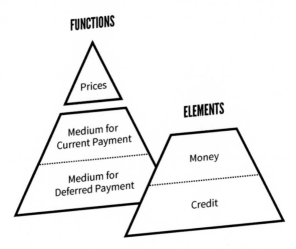

Figure 11.2 A financial system without banking: part one

Separating the Private from the Public Sphere

Figure 11.3 depicts how the private and the public sphere overlap in the organization of money and credit. On the one hand, by creating inside money, private institutions engage in the organization of money. Most of the money is supplied by private banking institutions. On the other hand, credit is not a completely private affair either, because banking institutions have their liabilities guaranteed by the government.

In today's banking system, the public sector takes on broad responsibilities not only for money but also for credit. It does so because banking institutions create money out of credit. Since credit affects the money supply, it affects the price system. Being responsible for price stability, the public sector is forced to adopt an important role in credit, too.

Having expanded their banking guarantees to shadow banking institutions, governments suppressed a correction of price distortions in the aftermath of the financial crisis of 2007–08. Without effective banking regulation in place, ever more credit needs to be guaranteed after every financial crisis by the government to safeguard the price system against the materialization of liquidity risk.

But the organization of credit cannot be built on suppressing risks forever, as it begins to affect the organization of money. The more inside money the government guarantees, the less credible becomes the promise of price stability. With more and more inside money guaranteed and no effective regulation in place, the ultimate correction of price distortions will be fiercer.

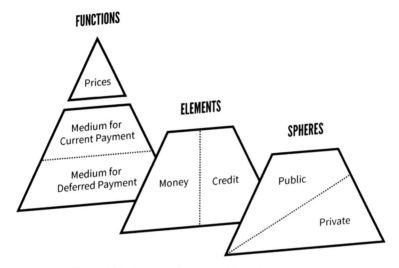

Figure 11.3 *A financial system with banking: part two*

The organization of credit needs to allow risks to be materialized, similar to a sensible wildfire policy that does not build on the principle of fire suppression at all cost.[4] The real economy always experiences ups and downs that cannot be foreseen. Credit—as a bilateral agreement between two parties—joins in the economic tide. The downward risks should be taken by those who also enjoy the possible upside benefits. A public sector interested in the long-term stability of a financial system needs to abstain from providing any guarantees to credit.

Under a systemic solvency rule, turmoil on credit markets will not result in banking panics anymore. Money is no longer created out of credit and government guarantees of credit can be credibly withdrawn. The monetary authority no longer faces situations where it has to sacrifice its primary goal of price stability. Being freed from any commitments regarding credit, the public sector can credibly commit to a functioning price system.

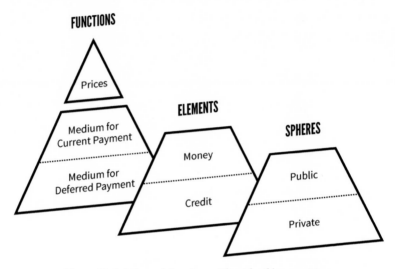

Figure 11.4 *A financial system without banking: part two*

We are now in a position to draw a clear line between the public and the private sector. Figure 11.4 illustrates this separation. While the organization of money belongs to the public sphere, credit is left to competitive forces and to be organized privately. Both the functional separation and the clear assignment of roles to the private and public sectors provide the foundation for a stable, effective, and fair financial system in the digital age.

---------------------------------- NOTES ----------------------------------

1. Haughwout et al. suggest (2012) that more than three million excess housing units were produced during the housing frenzy in the United States. In Europe, the picture looks similar. Spain, for instance, has been hit particularly hard by the crisis, with 14% of all properties vacant (Neate 2014).

2. The illusion of prosperity, which unrestricted banking creates, is sometimes used as an argument against banking regulations. Some economists claim that instability is the price for welfare, and that society would have to sacrifice economic growth if it were to constrain excessive risk taking. This argument is often brought forward in the context of capital requirements. Banking officials and lobbyists claim that higher capital requirements hurt the economy (see, e.g., the discussion in Admati and Hellwig 2013; Touryalai 2013). In some of the Goldman Sachs Global Investment Research reports, it is claimed that small and medium-sized enterprises (Ramsden et al. 2010) and low-income borrowers (Ramsden et al. 2011) suffer the most under higher capital requirements. Such arguments are flawed. The financial crisis of 2007–08 has forcefully confirmed that unrestricted banking only creates the illusion of prosperity, which eventually falls apart.

3. See Reinhart and Rogoff (2009a, 466) who have studied the negative effects of financial crises on output and employment. Unemployment rates rise on average by 7%, and output falls by 9% in the aftermath of financial crisis. One particularly damaging effect of the recent financial crisis has been the sharp rise in youth unemployment. As of 2009, almost 19% of the OECD area youth were unemployed (Scarpetta, Sonnet, and Manfredi 2010, 4). Affected young people are often scarred by unemployment because of its long-term negative effects on future wages and employability.

4. See Taleb (2012), who points out that suppressing volatility in complex social, political, and economic systems and in our own lives increases the likelihood of catastrophic events, so-called negative black swans. Similar thoughts have been formulated by Minsky (1986); the saying that "stability breeds instability" is attributed to him.

Conclusion

In the digital age, the financial system turned into a complex beast. Some of the best physicists, mathematicians, and lawyers work in modern banking. They speak a language and create products that are impossible to understand by outsiders. This makes it difficult to establish a political debate on financial reform.

Opacity is what prevented politicians from demanding radical changes after the financial crisis of 2007–08. Virtually everyone knows that banking got out of control, but where did the problems originate in this maze of financial products, institutions, and regulations? As long as even well-educated people have difficulty understanding what is happening behind the scenes, unconstrained banking will persist.

We hope we have succeeded in lifting the veil of modern finance. Behind numerous acronyms, we discerned banking, the creation of money out of credit. No matter what form banking takes, it comes with the same weaknesses. Once you reduce modern finance to its basic elements, the pieces fall into place. We can draw a line from the origins of banks and early banking panics to the rise and fall of shadow banking. The financial crisis of 2007–08 no longer seems to be a natural disaster or the inevitable result of human greed; it was the consequence of banking slipping out of control.

Current regulatory efforts cling to a notion of banking as it was practiced in the industrial age. They will not spare us the next financial crisis. The rise of information technology has undermined all efforts to regain control over banking.

At the same time, information technology enables a better organization of the financial system. We do not have to live with a broken banking system. It is time to demand the end of banking, for which only minor legal changes are needed. In particular, we have to add a systemic solvency rule to corporate law and adjust monetary policy.

Setting the legal framework for a new financial system without banking is simpler than unwinding the old banking system. Decades of unconstrained banking have created an inconceivable web of financial interdependencies. The transition to a financial system without banking might be a rocky road. For sure, it will involve uncertainty.

While we need to be aware of the risks in reforming the financial system, we cannot allow uncertainty to paralyze us. Sticking with banking is not an option. We should stop wasting resources on ever more complex banking regulation that will not prevent the next financial crisis. Banking is out of control, and instead of trying to fix it, we should prepare for the end of it.

In 2008, we were taken by surprise. We believed that there was no alternative, so we kicked the can down the road and kept a dysfunctional banking system on life support. We now know better: There is an alternative. It would be a shame if we were not prepared next time. Let us not waste another financial crisis. We can do better than banking.

References

Acharya, Viral V., and T. Sabri Öncü. 2010. "The Repurchase Agreement (Repo) Market." In *Regulating Wall Street: The Dodd-Frank Act and the New Architecture of Global Finance*, edited by Viral A. Acharya, Thomas F. Cooley, Matthew P. Richardson, and Ingo Walter, 319–50. New York: Wiley.

Acharya, Viral V., Philipp Schnabl, and Gustavo A. Suarez. 2013. "Securitization without Risk Transfer." *Journal of Financial Economics* 107 (3): 515–36.

Acharya, Viral V., and Tanju Yorulmazer. 2007. "Too Many to Fail—An Analysis of Time-Inconsistency in Bank Closure Policies." *Journal of Financial Intermediation* 16 (1): 1–31.

Admati, Anat R., Peter M. DeMarzo, Martin F. Hellwig, and Paul Pfleiderer. 2011. "Fallacies, Irrelevant Facts, and Myths in the Discussion of Capital Regulation: Why Bank Equity Is Not Expensive." Working Paper 86. Stanford, CA: The Rock Center for Corporate Governance at Stanford University. http://papers.ssrn.com/sol3/papers.cfm?abstract_id=1669704.

Admati, Anat R., and Martin F. Hellwig. 2013. *The Bankers' New Clothes: What's Wrong with Banking and What to Do about It.* Princeton, NJ: Princeton University Press.

Akerlof, George A. 1970. "The Market for 'Lemons': Quality Uncertainty and the Market Mechanism." *Quarterly Journal of Economics* 84 (3): 488–500.

Akerlof, George A., William T. Dickens, George L. Perry, Robert J. Gordon, and N. Gregory Mankiw. 1996. "The Macroeconomics of Low Inflation." *Brookings Papers on Economic Activity* 1996 (1): 1–76.

Alchian, Armen A., and Benjamin Klein. 1973. "On a Correct Measure of Inflation." *Journal of Money, Credit and Banking* 5 (1): 173–91.

Aliber, Robert Z. 1984. "International Banking: A Survey." *Journal of Money, Credit and Banking* 16 (4): 661–78.

Allen, Franklin, James McAndrews, and Philip Strahan. 2002. "E-Finance: An Introduction." *Journal of Financial Services Research* 22 (1–2): 5–27.

Allen, William R. 1993. "Irving Fisher and the 100 Percent Reserve Proposal." *Journal of Law and Economics* 36 (2): 703–17.

Altunbas, Yener, Leonardo Gambacorta, and David Marqués-Ibáñez. 2009. "Securitisation and the Bank Lending Channel." *European Economic Review* 53 (8): 996–1009.

Anderson, Richard G., and Charles S. Gascon. 2009. "The Commercial Paper Market, the Fed, and the 2007–2009 Financial Crisis." *Federal Reserve Bank of St. Louis Review* 91 (6): 589–612.

Anderson, Richard G., and Yang Liu. 2013. "How Low Can You Go? Negative Interest Rates and Investors' Flight to Safety." *Regional Economist* January: 12–13.

Andreessen, Marc. 2014. "Why Bitcoin Matters." *Deal Book, The New York Times,* January 21. http://dealbook.nytimes.com/2014/01/21/why-bitcoin-matters/.

Arlidge, John. 2009. "I'm Doing 'God's Work': Meet Mr. Goldman Sachs." *Sunday Times,* November 8. http://www.thesundaytimes.co.uk/sto/news/world_news/article189615.ece.

Arteta, Carlos, Mark Carey, Ricardo Correa, and Jason D. Kotter. 2013. "Revenge of the Steamroller: ABCP as a Window on Risk Choices." International Finance Discussion Papers 1076. Board of Governors of the Federal Reserve System. http://www.federalreserve.gov/pubs/ifdp/2013/1076/ifdp1076.pdf.

Baba, Nahoika, Robert N. McCauley, and Srichander Ramaswamy. 2009. "US Dollar Money Market Funds and Non-US Banks." *BIS Quarterly Review*, March, 65–81.

Bagehot, Walter. 1873. *Lombard Street: A Description of the Money Market.* London: Henry S. King.

Bair, Sheila. 2007. "Remarks By Sheila Bair Chairman, U.S. Federal Deposit Insurance Corporation." Speech presented at the 2007 Risk Management and Allocation Conference, Paris, France, June 25. http://www.fdic.gov/news/news/speeches/archives/2007/chairman/spjun2507.html.

Banerjee, Abhijit V., and Eric S. Maskin. 1996. "A Walrasian Theory of Money and Barter." *Quarterly Journal of Economics* 111 (4): 955–1005.

Bank for International Settlement. 2014. "OTC Derivatives Market Activity in the Second Half of 2013." Statistical Release. http://www.bis.org/publ/otc_hy1405.htm.

"Banking without Banks." *The Economist*, March 1, 2014. http://www.economist.com/news/finance-and-economics/21597932-offering-both-borrowers-and-lenders-better-deal-websites-put-two.

Barber, Simon, Xavier Boyen, Elaine Shi, and Ersin Uzun. 2012. "Bitter to Better—How to Make Bitcoin a Better Currency." In *Financial Cryptography and Data Security*, edited by Angelos D. Keromytis, 399–414. Lecture Notes in Computer Science 7397. Berlin: Springer.

Basel Committee on Banking Supervision. 1988. "International Convergence of Capital Measurement and Capital Standards." Basel: Bank for International Settlements. http://www.bis.org/publ/bcbs04a.htm.

———. 2004. "Basel II: International Convergence of Capital Measurement and Capital Standards: A Revised Framework." Basel: Bank for International Settlements. http://www.bis.org/publ/bcbs107.htm.

———. 2006. "Results of the Fifth Quantitative Impact Study (QIS 5)." Basel: Bank for International Settlements. http://www.bis.org/bcbs/qis/qis-5results.pdf.

———. 2009. "History of the Basel Committee." Basel: Bank for International Settlements. http://www.bis.org/bcbs/history.htm.

———. 2011. "Basel III: A Global Regulatory Framework for More Resilient Banks and Banking Systems—Revised Version June 2011." Basel: Bank for International Settlements. http://www.bis.org/publ/bcbs189.htm.

———. 2013. "Regulatory Consistency Assessment Programme (RCAP)—Analysis of Risk Weighted Assets for Market Risk." Basel: Bank for International Settlements. http://www.bis.org/publ/bcbs240.pdf.

Beck, Thorsten, Asli Demirgüç-Kunt, and Ross Levine. 2013. "A New Database on Financial Development and Structure." Data set. http://siteresources.worldbank.org/INTRES/Resources/469232-1107449512766/FinStructure_April_2013.xlsx.

Benes, Jaromir, and Michael Kumhof. 2012. "The Chicago Plan Revisited." IMF Working Paper 12/202. Washington: International Monetary Fund. http://www.imf.org/external/pubs/ft/wp/2012/wp12202.pdf.

Benmelech, Efraim, and Jennifer Dlugosz. 2010. "The Credit Rating Crisis." In *NBER Macroeconomics Annual 2009, Vol. 24*, edited by Daron Acemoglu, Kenneth Rogoff, and Michael Woodford, 161–207. Chicago: University of Chicago Press.

Benston, George J. 1994. "Universal Banking." *Journal of Economic Perspectives* 8 (3): 121–43.

Berger, Allen N., and W. Scott Frame. 2007. "Small Business Credit Scoring and Credit Availability." *Journal of Small Business Management* 45 (1): 5–22.

Berger, Allen N., and Gregory F. Udell. 2002. "Small Business Credit Availability and Relationship Lending: The Importance of Bank Organisational Structure." *Economic Journal* 112 (477): F32–F53.

Bernanke, Ben S. 2002. "Deflation—Making Sure 'It' Doesn't Happen Here." Speech presented at the National Economists Club, Washington, November 22. http://www.federalreserve.gov/boarddocs/speeches/2002/20021121/.

———. 2007. "The Subprime Mortgage Market." Speech presented at the Federal Reserve Bank of Chicago's 43rd Annual Conference on Bank Structure and Competition, Chicago, May 17. http://www.federalreserve.gov/newsevents/speech/bernanke20070517a.htm.

———. 2009. "The Crisis and the Policy Response." Speech presented at the Stamp Lecture, London School of Economics, London, January 13. http://www.federalreserve.gov/newsevents/speech/bernanke20090113a.htm.

Bessembinder, Hendrik, and William Maxwell. 2008. "Markets: Transparency and the Corporate Bond Market." *Journal of Economic Perspectives* 22 (2): 217–34.

Bessembinder, Hendrik, William Maxwell, and Kumar Venkataraman. 2006. "Market Transparency, Liquidity Externalities, and Institutional Trading Costs in Corporate Bonds." *Journal of Financial Economics* 82 (2): 251–88.

Bhattacharya, Sudipto, Arnoud W. A. Boot, and Anjan V. Thakor. 1998. "The Economics of Bank Regulation." *Journal of Money, Credit and Banking* 30 (4): 745–70.

Birdthistle, William A. 2010. "Breaking Bucks in Money Market Funds." *Wisconsin Law Review*, 1155–1200.

Bliss, Robert R., and George G. Kaufman. 2006. "Derivatives and Systemic Risk: Netting, Collateral, and Closeout." *Journal of Financial Stability* 2 (1): 55–70.

Block, Walter, and Kenneth M. Garschina. 1996. "Hayek, Business Cycles and Fractional Reserve Banking: Continuing the De-Homogenization Process." *Review of Austrian Economics* 9 (1): 77–94.

Blum, Jürg, and Martin Hellwig. 1995. "The Macroeconomic Implications of Capital Adequacy Requirements for Banks." *European Economic Review* 39 (3–4): 739–49.

Board of Governors of the Federal Reserve System. 2005. *The Federal Reserve System: Purposes & Functions.* 9th ed. Washington, DC. http://www.federalreserve.gov/pf/pdf/pf_complete.pdf.

———. 2009. Press Release. March 18. http://www.federalreserve.gov/newsevents/press/monetary/20090318a.htm.

Bossone, Biagio. 2001. "Should Banks Be Narrowed?" IMF Working Paper 01/159. http://www.imf.org/external/pubs/ft/wp/2001/wp01159.pdf.

Boyd, John H., and Mark Gertler. 1993. "U.S. Commercial Banking: Trends, Cycles, and Policy." In *NBER Macroeconomics Annual 1993, Vol. 8*, edited by Olivier Blanchard and Stanley Fischer, 319–77. Cambridge, MA: MIT Press.

Braithwaite, Tom, and Patrick Jenkins. 2011. "JPMorgan Chief Says Bank Rules 'Anti-US'." *Financial Times.* http://www.ft.com/intl/cms/s/0/905aeb88-dc50-11e0-8654-00144feabdc0.html#axzz1yDprYqHQ.

Bricker, Jesse, Arthur B. Kennickell, Kevin B. Moore, and John Sabelhaus. 2012. "Changes in U.S. Family Finances from 2007 to 2010: Evidence from the Survey of Consumer Finances." *Federal Reserve Bulletin* 98 (2): 1–80.

Brunnermeier, Markus K. 2009. "Deciphering the Liquidity and Credit Crunch 2007–2008." *Journal of Economic Perspectives* 23 (1): 77–100.

Brunnermeier, Markus K., Andrew Crockett, Charles A. E. Goodhart, Avinash D. Persaud and Hyun Shin. 2009. *The Fundamental Principles of Financial Regulation. Geneva Reports on the World Economy 11.* Geneva: International Center for Monetary and Banking Studies.

Bryant, John. 1980. "A Model of Reserves, Bank Runs, and Deposit Insurance." *Journal of Banking and Finance* 4 (4): 335–44.

Buiter, Willem H., and N. Panigirtzoglou. 2003. "Overcoming the Zero Bound on Nominal Interest Rates with Negative Interest on Currency: Gesell's Solution." *Economic Journal* 113: 723–46.

Buser, Stephen A., Andrew H. Chen, and Edward J. Kane. 1981. "Federal Deposit Insurance, Regulatory Policy, and Optimal Bank Capital." *Journal of Finance* 36 (1): 51–60.

Calomiris, Charles W., and Charles M. Kahn. 1991. "The Role of Demandable Debt in Structuring Optimal Banking Arrangements." *American Economic Review* 81 (3): 497–531.

Carlson, Mark A. 2013. "Lessons from the Historical Use of Reserve Requirements in the United States to Promote Bank Liquidity." Finance and Economics Discussion Series 2013–11. Divisions of Research and Statistics and Monetary Affairs. Washington, DC: Federal Reserve Board.   http://www.federalreserve.gov/pubs/feds/2013/201311/201311pap.pdf.

Carruthers, Bruce G., and Wendy Nelson Espeland. 1991. "Accounting for Rationality: Double-Entry Bookkeeping and the Rhetoric of Economic Rationality." *American Journal of Sociology* 97 (1): 31–69.

Chamley, Christophe, Laurence J. Kotlikoff, and Herakles Polemarchakis. 2012. "Limited-Purpose Banking—Moving from 'Trust Me' to 'Show Me' Banking." *American Economic Review* 102 (3): 113–19.

Chari, Varadarajan V., and Patrick J. Kehoe. 2013. "Bailouts, Time Inconsistency, and Optimal Regulation." NBER Working Paper 19192. National Bureau of Economic Research. http://www.nber.org/papers/w19192.

Chou, Robin K., and Huimin Chung. 2006. "Decimalization, Trading Costs, and Information Transmission between ETFs and Index Futures." *Journal of Futures Markets* 26 (2): 131–51.

Cook, Timothy Q., and Jeremy G. Duffield. 1979. "Money Market Mutual Funds: A Reaction to Government Regulations or a Lasting Financial Innovation?" *FRB Richmond Economic Review* (July–August): 15–31.

Coval, Joshua, Jakub Jurek, and Erik Stafford. 2009. "The Economics of Structured Finance." *Journal of Economic Perspectives* 23 (1): 3–25.

Covitz, Daniel M., Nellie Liang, and Gustavo A. Suarez. 2013. "The Evolution of a Financial Crisis: Collapse of the Asset-Backed Commercial Paper Market." *Journal of Finance* 68 (3): 815–48

Crotty, James. 2007. "If Financial Market Competition Is So Intense, Why Are Financial Firm Profits So High? Reflections on the Current "Golden Age" of Finance." Working Paper 134. Amherst, MA: Political Economy Research Institute, University of Massachusetts Amherst. http://people.umass.edu/crotty/WP134.pdf.

Danielsson, Jon, Paul Embrechts, Charles Goodhart, Con Keating, Felix Muennich, Olivier Renault, and Hyun Song Shin. 2001. "An Academic Response to Basel II." Special Paper 130. LSE Financial Markets Group. ftp://ftp.math.ethz.ch/hg/users/embrecht/Basel2.pdf.

De Jong, Abe, Rezaul Kabir, and Thuy Thu Nguyen. 2008. "Capital Structure around the World: The Roles of Firm- and Country-Specific Determinants." *Journal of Banking and Finance* 32 (9): 1954–69.

Demirgüç-Kunt, Asli, and Edward J. Kane. 2002. "Deposit Insurance around the Globe: Where Does It Work?" *Journal of Economic Perspectives* 16 (2): 175–95.

Demirgüç-Kunt, Asli, Edward J. Kane, and Luc Laeven. 2008. *Deposit Insurance around the World: Issues of Design and Implementation.* Cambridge, MA: MIT Press.

Demyanyk, Yuliya, and Otto Van Hemert. 2011. "Understanding the Subprime Mortgage Crisis." *Review of Financial Studies* 24 (6): 1848–80.

Dennis, Steven A., and Donald J. Mullineaux. 2000. "Syndicated Loans." *Journal of Financial Intermediation* 9 (4): 404–26.

Dewatripont, Mathias, and Jean Tirole. 1994. "A Theory of Debt and Equity: Diversity of Securities and Manager-Shareholder Congruence." *Quarterly Journal of Economics* 109 (4): 1027–54.

Diamond, Douglas W., and Philip H. Dybvig. 1983. "Bank Runs, Deposit Insurance, and Liquidity." *Journal of Political Economy* 91 (3): 401–19.

Diamond, Douglas W., and Raghuram G. Rajan. 2001. "Liquidity Risk, Liquidity Creation and Financial Fragility: A Theory of Banking." *Journal of Political Economy* 109 (2): 287–327.

Domowitz, Ian. 2002. "Liquidity, Transaction Costs, and Reintermediation in Electronic Markets." *Journal of Financial Services Research* 22 (1-2): 141–57.

Duffie, Darrell, Nicolae Gârleanu, and Lasse Heje Pedersen. 2005. "Over-the-Counter Markets." *Econometrica* 73 (6): 1815–47.

Dynan, Karen E., Douglas W. Elmendorf, and Daniel E. Sichel. 2006. "Can Financial Innovation Help to Explain the Reduced Volatility of Economic Activity?" *Journal of Monetary Economics* 53 (1): 123–50.

eBay Inc. 2014. *eBay Marketplaces Fast Facts At-A-Glance (Q1 2014).* http://www.ebayinc.com/system/download_links/MP%20Factsheet%20Q1%20 2014.pdf?download=1.

Estrella, Arturo. 2002. "Securitization and the Efficacy of Monetary Policy." *FRBNY Economic Policy Review* 8 (1): 241–55.

Fama, Eugene F. 1980. "Banking in the Theory of Finance." *Journal of Monetary Economics* 6 (1): 39–57.

Farhi, Emmanuel, and Jean Tirole. 2012. "Collective Moral Hazard, Maturity Mismatch, and Systemic Bailouts." *American Economic Review* 102 (1): 60–93.

Federal Deposit Insurance Corporation. 1984. *FDIC: The First Fifty Years—A History of the FDIC 1933–1983.* http://www.fdic.gov/bank/analytical/firstfifty/.

———. 2010. "About FDIC—The 1930's." http://www.fdic.gov/about/history/timeline/1930s.html.

Federal Reserve Bank of New York. 2010. "Administration of Relationships with Primary Dealers." http://www.newyorkfed.org/markets/pridealers_policies.html.

———. 2014. "Primary Dealers List." http://www.newyorkfed.org/markets/pridealers_current.html.

Fettig, David. 2002. "Lender of More Than Last Resort." *The Region—The Federal Reserve Bank of Minneapolis,* December. http://www.minneapolisfed.org/publications_papers/pub_display.cfm?id=3392&.

———. 2008. "The History of a Powerful Paragraph." *The Region—The Federal Reserve Bank of Minneapolis,* June. https://www.minneapolisfed.org/publications_papers/pub_display.cfm?id=3485.

Fischer, Stanley. 1996. "Why Are Central Banks Pursuing Long-Run Price Stability?" Paper presented at Achieving Price Stability, a symposium sponsored by the Federal Reserve Bank of Kansas City, Jackson Hole, WY, August 29–31. http://www.kc.frb.org/publications/research/escp/escp-1996.cfm.

———. 1999. "On the Need for an International Lender of Last Resort." *Journal of Economic Perspectives* 13 (4): 85–104.

Fisher, Irving. 1933a. "The Debt-Deflation Theory of Great Depressions." *Econometrica* 1 (4): 337–57.

———. 1933b. *Stamp Scrip.* New York: Adelphi.

———. 1935. *100% Money.* New York: Adelphi.

Freixas, Xavier, and Jean-Charles Rochet. 2008. *Microeconomics of Banking.* Cambridge, MA: MIT Press.

French, George. 2004. "Estimating the Capital Impact of Basel II in the United States." Federal Deposit Insurance Corporation. http://www.fdic.gov/bank/analytical/fyi/2003/120803fyi.html.

Friedman, Benjamin M. 1999. "The Future of Monetary Policy: The Central Bank as an Army with Only a Signal Corps?" *International Finance* 2 (3): 321–38.

———. 2000. "Decoupling at the Margin: The Threat to Monetary Policy from the Electronic Revolution in Banking." *International Finance* 3 (2): 261–72.

Friedman, Milton. 1948. "A Monetary and Fiscal Framework for Economic Stability." *American Economic Review* 38 (3): 245–64.

———. 1965. *A Program for Monetary Stability.* 4th ed. New York: Fordham University Press.

Friedman, Milton, and Anna J. Schwartz. 1986. "Has Government Any Role in Money?" *Journal of Monetary Economics* 17 (1): 37–62.

Gerschenkron, Alexander. 1962. *Economic Backwardness in Historical Perspective.* Cambridge, MA: Harvard University Press.

Gesell, Silvio. 1916. *Die natürliche Wirtschaftsordnung durch Freiland und Freigeld [The Natural Economic Order].* Les Hauts Geneveys: Verlag Silvio Gesell.

Goodfriend, Marvin. 2000. "Overcoming the Zero Bound on Interest Rate Policy." *Journal of Money, Credit and Banking* 32 (4): 1007–35.

———. 2011. "Central Banking in the Credit Turmoil: An Assessment of Federal Reserve Practice." *Journal of Monetary Economics* 58 (1): 1–12.

Goodhart, Charles. 2001. "What Weight Should Be Given to Asset Prices in the Measurement of Inflation?" *Economic Journal* 111 (472): 335–56.

———. 2008. "The Boundary Problem in Financial Regulation." *National Institute Economic Review* 206 (1): 48–55.

Goodman, Lawrence. 2012. "Demand for U.S. Debt Is Not Limitless." *Wall Street Journal.* http://online.wsj.com/news/articles/SB10001424052702304450004577279754275393064.

Gorton, Gary, Stefan Lewellen, and Andrew Metrick. 2012. "The Safe-Asset Share." *American Economic Review* 102 (3): 101–6.

Gorton, Gary, and Andrew Metrick. 2010. "Haircuts." *Federal Reserve Bank of St. Louis Review* 92 (6): 507–19. https://research.stlouisfed.org/publications/review/10/11/Gorton.pdf.

———. 2012. "Securitized Banking and the Run on Repo." *Journal of Financial Economics* 104 (3): 425–51.

Gorton, Gary, and George Pennacchi. 1990. "Financial Intermediaries and Liquidity Creation." *Journal of Finance* 45 (1): 49–71.

Gorton, Gary B. 2010. *Slapped by the Invisible Hand: The Panic of 2007.* Oxford: Oxford University Press.

Gorton, Gary B., and Nicholas S. Souleles. 2007. "Special Purpose Vehicles and Securitization." In *The Risks of Financial Institutions,* edited by Mark Carey and René M. Stulz, 549–602. Chicago: University of Chicago Press.

Gorton, Gary B., and Andrew Winton. 2003. "Financial Intermediation." In *Handbook of the Economics of Finance, Vol. 1A: Corporate Finance,* edited by G. M. Constantinides, M. Harris, and R. M. Stulz, 431–552. Amsterdam: Elsevier.

Greenspan, Alan. 1998. "The Role of Capital in Optimal Banking Supervision and Regulation." *FRBNY Economic Policy Review* 4 (3): 163–68.

———. 2009. "The Fed Didn't Cause the Housing Bubble." *Wall Street Journal Online*, November 3. http://iepecdg.com.br/Arquivos/ Leiturassugeridas/090311_greenspan_fed_housing_bubble.pdf.

Gropp, Reint, Christian Gruendl, and Andre Guettler. 2014. "The Impact of Public Guarantees on Bank Risk-Taking: Evidence from a Natural Experiment." *Review of Finance* 18 (2): 457–88.

Grossman, Richard S. 1992. "Deposit Insurance, Regulation, and Moral Hazard in the Thrift Industry: Evidence from the 1930's." *American Economic Review* 82 (4): 800–821.

Grove, William M, and Paul E. Meehl. 1996. "Comparative Efficiency of Informal (Subjective, Impressionistic) and Formal (Mechanical, Algorithmic) Prediction Procedures: The Clinical-Statistical Controversy." *Psychology, Public Policy and Law* 2 (2): 293–323.

Haldane, Andrew G. 2012a. "On Being the Right Size." Speech presented at the Institute of Economic Affairs 22nd Annual Series, 2012 Beesley Lectures, Pall Mall, October 25. http://www.bankofengland.co.uk/ publications/Documents/speeches/2012/speech615.pdf.

———. 2012b. "Towards a Common Financial Language." Paper presented at the Securities Industry and Financial Markets Association (SIFMA) "Building a Global Legal Entity Identifier Framework" Symposium, New York, March 14.

Haldane, Andrew G., and Vasileios Madouros. 2012. "The Dog and the Frisbee." Speech presented at the Federal Reserve Bank of Kansas City's 36th Economic Policy Symposium, The Changing Policy Landscape, Jackson Hole, WY, August 31.

Hancock, Diana, and David B. Humphrey. 1998. "Payment Transactions, Instruments, and Systems: A Survey." *Journal of Banking and Finance* 21: 1573–624.

Hannoun, Hervé, and Boris Hofman. 2012. "Monetary Policy in the Crisis: Testing the Limits of Monetary Policy." Speech by Hervé Hannoun presented at the 47th SEACON Governors' Conference, Seoul, Korea, February 13–14. http://www.bis.org/speeches/sp120216.pdf.

Hanson, Samuel G., Anil K. Kashyap, and Jeremy C. Stein. 2011. "A Macroprudential Approach to Financial Regulation." *Journal of Economic Perspectives* 25 (1): 3–28.

Haubrich, Joseph G., and Paul Wachtel. 1993. "Capital Requirements and Shifts in Commercial Bank Portfolios." *Economic Review—Federal Reserve Bank of Cleveland* 29 (3): 2–15.

Haughwout, Andrew, Richard W. Peach, John Sporn, and Joseph Tracy. 2012. *The Supply Side of the Housing Boom and Bust of the 2000s.* Staff Report 556. New York: Federal Reserve Bank of New York.

Hayek, Friedrich August. 1945. "The Use of Knowledge in Society." *American Economic Review* 35 (4): 519–30.

Hellwig, Martin. 1991. "Banking, Financial Intermediation, and Corporate Finance." In *European Financial Integration*, edited by Alberto Giovannini and Colin Mayer, 35–63. Cambridge: Cambridge University Press.

Hendershott, Terrence, Charles M. Jones, and Albert J. Menkveld. 2011. "Does Algorithmic Trading Improve Liquidity?" *Journal of Finance* 66 (1): 1–33.

Hill, Claire A. 2004. "Regulating the Rating Agencies." *Washington University Law Review* 82 (1): 43–94.

———. 2009. "Why Did Rating Agencies Do Such a Bad Job Rating Subprime Securities?" *University of Pittsburgh Law Review* 71 (3): 585–608.

Holmström, Bengt, and Jean Tirole. 1997. "Financial Intermediation, Loanable Funds, and the Real Sector." *Quarterly Journal of Economics* 112 (3): 663–91.

Huber, Joseph, and James Robertson. 2000. *Creating New Money: A Monetary Reform for the Information Age.* London: New Economics Foundation.

Huerta de Soto, Jesús, and Melinda A Stroup. 2009. *Money, Bank Credit, and Economic Cycles.* Auburn, AL: Ludwig von Mises Institute.

Humphrey, David, Magnus Willesson, Ted Lindblom, and Göran Bergendahl. 2003. "What Does It Cost to Make a Payment?" *Review of Network Economics* 2 (2): 159–74.

Ivashina, Victoria, and David Scharfstein. 2010. "Bank Lending during the Financial Crisis of 2008." *Journal of Financial Economics* 97 (3): 319–38.

Jacklin, Charles J. 1987. "Demand Deposits, Trading Restrictions, and Risk-Sharing." In *Contractual Arrangements for Intertemporal Trade*, edited by Edward Prescott and Neil Wallace, 26–47. Minneapolis: University of Minnesota Press.

Jackson, Andrew, Ben Dyson, and Graham Hodgson. 2013. *The Positive Money Proposal.* http://www.positivemoney.org/wp-content/uploads/2013/04/The-Positive-Money-Proposal-2nd-April-2013.pdf.

Jackson, Patricia, Craig Furfine, Hans Groeneveld, Diana Hancock, David Jones, William Perraudin, Lawrence Radecki, and Masao Yoneyama. 1999. "Capital Requirements and Bank Behaviour: The Impact of the Basle Accord." Basel Committee on Banking Supervision Working Paper 1. Basel: Bank for International Settlements. http://www.bis.org/publ/bcbs_wp1.pdf.

Jiang, Wei, Ashlyn Aiko Nelson, and Edward Vytlacil. 2014. "Securitization and Loan Performance: Ex Ante and Ex Post Relations in the Mortgage Market." *Review of Financial Studies* 27 (2): 454–83.

Johnson, Roger T. 2010. *Historical Beginnings, the Federal Reserve*. Boston: Public and Community Affairs Department, Federal Reserve Bank of Boston. https://www.bostonfed.org/about/pubs/begin.pdf.

Jones, Claire. 2014. "ECB Unveils Radical Moves to Fight Deflation and Lift Economy." *Financial Times*, June 5. http://www.ft.com/intl/cms/s/0/fd55cd1a-ec98-11e3-a754-00144feabdc0.html?siteedition=uk.

Jones, David. 2000. "Emerging Problems with the Basel Capital Accord: Regulatory Capital Arbitrage and Related Issues." *Journal of Banking and Finance* 24 (1): 35–58.

Kane, Edward J. 1981. "Accelerating Inflation, Technological Innovation, and the Decreasing Effectiveness of Banking Regulation." *Journal of Finance* 36 (2): 355–67.

Kapstein, Ethan B. 1989. "Resolving the Regulator's Dilemma: International Coordination of Banking Regulations." *International Organization* 43 (2): 323–47.

Kareken, John H., and Neil Wallace. 1978. "Deposit Insurance and Bank Regulation: A Partial-Equilibrium Exposition." *Journal of Business* 51 (3): 413–38.

Kashyap, Anil K., and Jeremy C. Stein. 2004. "Cyclical Implications of the Basel II Capital Standards." *Economic Perspectives* 28 (1): 18–31.

Keys, Benjamin J., Amit Seru, and Vikrant Vig. 2012. "Lender Screening and the Role of Securitization: Evidence from Prime and Subprime Mortgage Markets." *Review of Financial Studies* 25 (7): 2071–108.

Kim, Daesik, and Anthony M. Santomero. 1988. "Risk in Banking and Capital Regulation." *Journal of Finance* 43 (5): 1219–33.

Kindleberger, Charles P. 1993. *A Financial History of Western Europe*. 2nd ed. New York: Oxford University Press.

Kindleberger, Charles P., and Robert Z. Aliber. 2005. *Manias, Panics, and Crashes: A History of Financial Crises*. 5th ed. Wiley Investment Classics. Hoboken, NJ: Wiley.

King, Mervyn. 2004. "The Institutions of Monetary Policy." *American Economic Review* 94 (2): 1–13.

King, Michael R., and Rime Dagfinn. 2010. "The $4 Trillion Question: What Explains FX Growth since the 2007 Survey?" *BIS Quarterly Review* (December): 27–42. http://www.bis.org/publ/qtrpdf/r_qt1012e.pdf.

King, Robert G., and Ross Levine. 1993. "Finance and Growth: Schumpeter Might Be Right." *Quarterly Journal of Economics* 108 (3): 717–37.

Kiyotaki, Nobuhiro, and Randall Wright. 1989. "On Money as a Medium of Exchange." *Journal of Political Economy* 97 (4): 927–54.

Kotlikoff, Laurence J. 2010. *Jimmy Stewart Is Dead: Ending the World's Ongoing Financial Plague with Limited Purpose Banking.* Hoboken, NJ: Wiley.

Krantz, Matt. 2014. "Downgrade! Only 3 U.S. Companies Now Rated AAA." *America's Markets, USA Today.* http://americasmarkets.usatoday. com/2014/04/11/downgrade-only-3-u-s-companies-now-rated-aaa/.

Kress, Jeremy C. 2011. "Credit Default Swap Clearinghouses and Systemic Risk: Why Centralized Counterparties Must Have Access to Central Bank Liquidity." *Harvard Journal on Legislation* 48 (1): 49–93.

Krishnamurthy, Arvind, and Annette Vissing-Jorgensen. 2011. "The Effects of Quantitative Easing on Interest Rates: Channels and Implications for Policy." NBER Working Paper 17555. National Bureau of Economic Research. http://www.nber.org/papers/w17555.

Lagos, Ricardo. 2010. "Asset Prices and Liquidity in an Exchange Economy." *Journal of Monetary Economics* 57 (8): 913–30.

Lagos, Ricardo, and Randall Wright. 2005. "A Unified Framework for Monetary Theory and Policy Analysis." *Journal of Political Economy* 113 (3): 463–84.

Lange, Oskar. 1936. "On the Economic Theory of Socialism: Part One." *Review of Economic Studies* 4 (1): 53–71.

Levine, Ross. 1997. "Financial Development and Economic Growth: Views and Agenda." *Journal of Economic Literature* 35 (2): 688–726.

Levine, Ross, and Sara Zervos. 1998. "Stock Markets, Banks, and Economic Growth." *American Economic Review* 88 (3): 537–58.

Lewis, Michael. 2011. *The Big Short : Inside the Doomsday Machine.* London: Penguin.

———. 2014. *Flash Boys: A Wall Street Revolt.* New York: Norton.

Lucas, Robert E., Jr. 2000. "Inflation and Welfare." *Econometrica* 68 (2): 247–74.

Macey, Jonathan. 2011. "Reducing Systemic Risk: The Role of Money Market Mutual Funds as Substitutes for Federally Insured Bank Deposits." *Stanford Journal of Law, Business and Finance* 17 (1): 131.

Mailath, George J., and Loretta J. Mester. 1994. "A Positive Analysis of Bank Closure." *Journal of Financial Intermediation* 3 (3): 272–99.

Mankiw, Gregory. 2009. "It May Be Time for the FED to Go Negative." *New York Times,* April 19. http://www.nytimes.com/2009/04/19/business/ economy/19view.html?_r=0.

Massad, Timothy G. 2011. "Acting Assistant Secretary Timothy G. Massad Written Testimony Before the Congressional Oversight Panel." U.S. Department of the Treasury. http://www.treasury.gov/press-center/ press-releases/Pages/tg1091.aspx.

Mayer, Colin. 1990. "Financial Systems, Corporate Finance, and Economic Development." In *Asymmetric Information, Corporate Finance, and*

Investment, edited by R. Glenn Hubbard, 307–32. Chicago: University of Chicago Press.

McLeay, Michael, Amar Radia, and Ryland Thomas. 2014. "Money Creation in the Modern Economy." *Quarterly Bulletin* 54 (1): 14–22.

Mehrling, Perry. 2011. *The New Lombard Street: How the Fed Became the Dealer of Last Resort.* Princeton, NJ: Princeton University Press.

Menger, Karl. 1892. "On the Origins of Money." *Economic Journal* 2 (6): 239–55.

Minsky, Hyman P. 1986. *Stabilizing an Unstable Economy.* New Haven, CT: Yale University Press.

Mises, Ludwig von. 1920. "Die Wirtschaftsrechnung Im Sozialistischen Gemeinwesen" [Economic Calculation in the Socialist Commonwealth]. *Archiv Für Sozialwissenschaften* 47: 86–121.

Mishkin, Frederic S. 1996. "The Channels of Monetary Transmission: Lessons for Monetary Policy." NBER Working Paper 5464. National Bureau of Economic Research. http://www.nber.org/papers/w5464.

Modigliani, Franco, and Merton H. Miller. 1958. "The Cost of Capital, Corporation Finance and the Theory of Investment." *American Economic Review* 48 (3): 261–97.

Nakamoto, Satoshi. 2008. "Bitcoin: A Peer-to-Peer Electronic Cash System." Unpublished report. http://bitcoin.org/bitcoin.pdf.

Nasiripour, Shahien, and Kara Scanell. 2013. "Holder Says Some Banks Are 'Too Large.'" *Financial Times,* July 3. http://www.ft.com/intl/cms/s/0/ecb0ced2-86b0-11e2-b907-00144feabdc0.html#axzz2lDoMqzlF.

Neate, Rupert. 2014. "Scandal of Europe's 11m Empty Homes." *The Guardian,* February 23. http://www.theguardian.com/society/2014/feb/23/europe-11m-empty-properties-enough-house-homeless-continent-twice.

Nersisyan, Yeva, and L. Randall Wray. 2010. "The Global Financial Crisis and the Shift to Shadow Banking." Working Paper 587. Annandale-on-Hudson, NY: Levy Economics Institute of Bard College. http://www.levyinstitute.org/pubs/wp_587.pdf

Noss, Joseph, and Rhiannon Sowerbutts. 2012. "The Implicit Subsidy of Banks." Bank of England Financial Stability Paper 15. London: Bank of England. http://hb.betterregulation.com/external/FS%20Paper%20No.%2015%20-%20The%20implicit%20subsidy%20of%20banks.pdf.

O'Driscoll, Gerald P. 2010. "Book Review: *Jimmy Stewart Is Dead: Ending the World's Ongoing Financial Plague with Limited Purpose Banking.*" *Cato Journal* 30 (3): 541–46.

O'Hara, Maureen, and Wayne Shaw. 1990. "Deposit Insurance and Wealth Effects: The Value of Being 'Too Big to Fail.'" *Journal of Finance* 45 (5): 1587–600.

Orticelli, Bryan J. 2009. "Crisis Compounded by Constraint: How Regulatory Inadequacies Impaired the Fed's Bailout of Bear Stearns." *Connecticut Law Review* 42 (2): 647–91.

P2P Finance Association. 2013. "Peer-to-Peer Finance Association Operating Principles (Updated July 2, 2013)." http://www.p2pfinanceassociation. org.uk/wp-content/uploads/2011/08/P2PFA-Operating-Principles.pdf.

Petersen, Mitchell A. 2004. "Information: Hard and Soft." Working Paper. Kellogg School of Management Northwestern University. http://www. kellogg.northwestern.edu/faculty/petersen/htm/papers/softhard.pdf.

Petersen, Mitchell A., and Raghuram G. Rajan. 2002. "Does Distance Still Matter? The Information Revolution in Small Business Lending." *Journal of Finance* 57 (6): 2533–70.

Philippon, Thomas, and Ariell Reshef. 2012. "Wages and Human Capital in the U.S. Finance Industry: 1909–2006." *Quarterly Journal of Economics* 127 (4): 1551–1609.

Plosser, Charles I. 2010. "Credible Commitments and Monetary Policy After the Crisis." Speech presented at the Swiss National Bank Monetary Policy Conference, Zurich, Switzerland, September 24. http://www. philadelphiafed.org/publications/speeches/plosser/2010/09-24-10_ swiss-national-bank.cfm.

———. 2012. "Fiscal Policy and Monetary Policy: Restoring the Boundaries." Speech presented at the U.S. Monetary Policy Forum, University of Chicago Booth School of Business, New York, February 24. http:// www.bis.org/review/r120228a.pdf.

Pollack, Lisa. 2013. "Ten Times on the Board: I Will Not Put 'Optimizing Regulatory Capital' in the Subject Line of an Email." *FT Alphaville.* http:// ftalphaville.ft.com/2013/04/09/1450202/ten-times-on-the-board-i-will-not-put-optimizing-regulatory-capital-in-the-subject-line-of-an-email/.

Pope, Theodore W., Peter T. Ender, William K. Woelk, Michael A. Koroscil, and Thomas M. Koroscil. 2002. "Bacterial Contamination of Paper Currency." *Southern Medical Journal* 95 (12): 1408–10.

Pozsar, Zoltan, Tobias Adrian, Adam Ashcraft, and Hayley Boesky. 2010. "Shadow Banking." Federal Reserve Bank of New York Staff Report 458. New York: Federal Reserve Bank of New York.

———. 2013. "Shadow Banking." *FRBNY Economic Policy Review* 19 (2): 1–16.

Preparata, Guido Giacomo, and John E. Elliott. 2004. "Free-Economics: The Vision of Reformer Silvio Gesell." *International Journal of Social Economics* 31 (10): 923–54.

Rajan, Raghuram G. 1998. "The Past and Future of Commercial Banking Viewed through an Incomplete Contract Lens." *Journal of Money, Credit and Banking* 30 (3): 524–50.

———. 2006. "Has Finance Made the World Riskier?" *European Financial Management* 12 (4): 499–533.

Rajan, Raghuram G., and Luigi Zingales. 1995. "What Do We Know about Capital Structure? Some Evidence from International Data." *Journal of Finance* 50 (5): 1421–60.

Ramsden, Richard, Charles P. Himmelberg, David Greely, and Anne Brennan. 2010. "Higher Capital Costs Hinder Loan Growth." Global Investment Research. New York: Goldman Sachs. http://www.goldmansachs.com/our-thinking/archive/higher-capital-costs.pdf.

Ramsden, Richard, Julio Quinteros Jr., John T. Williams, Matthew J. Fassler, Adrianne Shapira, and Patrick Archambault. 2011. "Higher Bank Costs Are Affecting Low-Income Borrowers Most." Global Investment Research. New York: Goldman Sachs. http://www.goldmansachs.com/our-thinking/public-policy/regulatory-reform/higher-bank-costs.pdf.

Reinhart, Carmen M., and Kenneth S. Rogoff. 2009a. "The Aftermath of Financial Crises." *American Economic Review* 99 (2): 466–72.

———. 2009b. *This Time Is Different: Eight Centuries of Financial Folly*. Princeton, NJ: Princeton University Press.

Repullo, Rafael, and Javier Suarez. 2013. "The Procyclical Effects of Bank Capital Regulation." *Review of Financial Studies* 26 (2): 452–90.

Richards, R. D. 1929. *The Early History of Banking in England*. New York: Augustus M. Kelley.

Rosenberg, Richard M., and Ronald B. Given. 1987. "Financially Troubled Banks: Private Solutions and Regulatory Alternatives." *Banking Law Journal* 104: 284.

Sapienza, Paola. 2002. "What Do State-Owned Firms Maximize? Evidence from the Italian Banks." CEPR Discussion Paper 3168. Centre for Economic Policy Research.

Scarpetta, Stefano, Anne Sonnet, and Thomas Manfredi. 2010. "Rising Youth Unemployment during the Crisis: How to Prevent Negative Long-Term Consequences on a Generation?" OECD Social, Employment, and Migration Working Paper 106. OECD Publishing. http://www.oecd-ilibrary.org/social-issues-migration-health/rising-youth-unemployment-during-the-crisis_5kmh79zb2mmv-en.

Scholtes, Saskia, and Richard Beales. 2007. "Top Rating Proving Crucial to Structured Finance Sector." *Financial Times*, May 17. http://www.ft.com/cms/s/0/21e5032e-0413-11dc-a931-000b5df10621.html.

Schumpeter, Joseph A. 1926. *Theorie der wirtschaftlichen Entwicklung : Eine Untersuchung über Unternehmergewinn, Kapital, Kredit, Zins und den Konjunkturzyklus*, 2nd ed. [The Theory of Economic Development: An

Inquiry into Profits, Capital, Credit, Interest, and the Business Cycle]. Munich: Duncker & Humblot.

———. 1950. *Capitalism, Socialism, and Democracy*. 3rd ed. New York: Harper and Brothers.

Schwartz, Anna J. 1992. "The Misuse of the Fed's Discount Window." *Federal Reserve Bank of St. Louis Review* 74 (5): 58–69.

Shin, Hyun Song. 2009. "Reflections on Northern Rock: The Bank Run That Heralded the Global Financial Crisis." *Journal of Economic Perspectives* 23 (1): 101–19.

Sieg, Linda, and Kiyoshi Takenaka. 2012. "Japan's Abe Taps Allies for Cabinet, Eyes Deflation." *Reuters*, December 26. http://www.reuters.com/article/2012/12/26/japan-politics-idUSL4N0A00CN20121226.

Silber, William L. 2009. "Why Did FDR's Bank Holiday Succeed?" *FRBNY Economic Policy Review* 15 (1): 19–30.

Simons, Henry C. 1936. "Rules versus Authorities in Monetary Policy." *Journal of Political Economy* 44 (1): 1–30.

Singh, Manhoman. 2010. "Collateral, Netting and Systemic Risk in the OTC Derivatives Market." IMF Working Paper 10/99. Washington: International Monetary Fund. http://www.imf.org/external/pubs/ft/wp/2010/wp1099.pdf.

Sjostrom, William K., Jr. 2009. "The AIG Bailout." *Washington and Lee Law Review* 66 (3): 943.

Starr, Ross M., and Joseph M. Ostroy. 1974. "Money and the Decentralization of Exchange." *Econometrica* 42 (6): 1093–113.

Stiglitz, Joseph E., and Andrew Weiss. 1981. "Credit Rationing in Markets with Imperfect Information." *American Economic Review* 71 (3): 393–410.

Summers, Lawrence. 1991. "How Should Long-Term Monetary Policy Be Determined?" *Journal of Money, Credit and Banking* 23 (3): 625–31.

Taleb, Nassim N. 2007. *The Black Swan: The Impact of the Highly Improbable*. New York: Random House.

———. 2012. *Antifragile: Things That Gain from Disorder*. New York: Random House.

Taylor, John B. 2001. "Expectations, Open Market Operations, and Changes in the Federal Funds Rate." *Federal Reserve Bank of St. Louis Review* 83 (4): 33–48.

Thomas, Lyn C. 2000. "A Survey of Credit and Behavioural Scoring: Forecasting Financial Risk of Lending to Consumers." *International Journal of Forecasting* 16 (2): 149–72.

Tobin, James. 1985. "Financial Innovation and Deregulation in Perspective." *Cowles Foundation Paper* 635: 19–29.

———. 1987. "A Case for Preserving Regulatory Distinctions." *Challenge* 30 (5): 10–17.

Touryalai, Halah. 2013. "Big Banks Warn Regulators: Tougher Capital Rules Will Hurt Everyone." *Forbes*. http://www.forbes.com/sites/halahtouryalai/2013/07/09/big-banks-warn-regulators-tougher-capital-rules-will-hurt-everyone/.

"Treasury's Paulson—Subprime Woes Likely Contained." *Reuters*, April 20, 2007. http://uk.reuters.com/article/2007/04/20/usa-subprime-paulson-idUKWBT00686520070420.

U.S. Bureau of Economic Analysis. 2013. "Table 6.16B. Corporate Profits by Industry." Last Revised on August 7, 2013. http://www.bea.gov/iTable/iTable.cfm?ReqID=9&step=1#reqid=9&step=3&isuri=1&903=237.

———. 2014. "Table 6.16D. Corporate Profits by Industry." Last Revised on June 25, 2014. http://www.bea.gov/iTable/iTable.cfm?ReqID=9&step=1#reqid=9&step=3&isuri=1&903=239.

U.S. Securities and Exchange Commission (SEC). 2008. "Summary Report of Issues Identified in the Commission Staff's Examination of Select Credit Rating Agencies." http://www.sec.gov/news/studies/2008/craexamination070808.pdf.

U.S. Senate Permanent Subcommittee on Investigations. 2013. "JPMorgan Chase Whale Trades: A Case History of Derivatives Risks and Abuses." Majority and Minority Staff Report. U.S. Senate. http://www.hsgac.senate.gov/download/report-jpmorgan-chase-whale-trades-a-case-history-of-derivatives-risks-and-abuses-march-15-2013.

Van Duyn, Aline, Deborah Brewster, and Gillian Tett. 2008. "The Lehman Legacy: Catalyst of the Crisis." *Financial Times*, December 10. http://www.ft.com/intl/cms/s/0/ea92428c-9887-11dd-ace3-000077b07658.html#axzz1z5Fzs52s.

Von Thadden, Ernst-Ludwig. 1998. "Intermediated versus Direct Investment: Optimal Liquidity Provision and Dynamic Incentive Compatibility." *Journal of Financial Intermediation* 7 (2): 177–97.

Wall, Larry D., and David R. Peterson. 1990. "The Effect of Continental Illinois' Failure on the Financial Performance of Other Banks." *Journal of Monetary Economics* 26 (1): 77–99.

Wallace, Neil. 1996. "Narrow Banking Meets the Diamond Dybvig Model." *Federal Reserve Bank of Minneapolis Quarterly Review* 20 (1): 3–13.

Walter, John R. 2006. "The 3-6-3 Rule: An Urban Myth?" *Federal Reserve Bank of Richmond Economic Quarterly* 92 (1): 51–78.

White, Lawrence J. 2010. "Markets: The Credit Rating Agencies." *Journal of Economic Perspectives* 24 (2): 211–26.

Wright, Richard, Erdal Tekin, Volkan Topalli, Chandler McClellan, Timothy Dickinson, and Richard Rosenfeld. 2014. "Less Cash, Less Crime: Evidence from the Electronic Benefit Transfer Program." NBER Working

Paper 19996. National Bureau of Economic Research. http://www.
nber.org/papers/w19996.

Index

Page references followed by *fig* indicate an illustrated figure; followed by *t* indicate a table.

About the Author

Jonathan McMillan is a pseudonym. Behind it stands an unlikely pair: a macroeconomist and an investment banker. They met while attending university, but lost touch with each other in the years after. One dived into academic research, where he specialized in the macroeconomic modeling of banks. The other started a career in investment banking and experienced firsthand the world of modern finance with its opaque products.

In 2011, their paths crossed again in a London pub, where they decided to set forth on a writing journey. In *The End of Banking*, they share their complementary insights into the workings of banking. They now live on different continents but are still joined in their fascination with the financial system. They try to meet up as often as possible to discuss latest developments in finance and, of course, to share a good time.

For further information, please visit
www.endofbanking.org

www.endofbanking.org

Lightning Source UK Ltd.
Milton Keynes UK
UKOW04f1658240116

267013UK00001B/49/P